KINGS

OF THE

STREET

PUBLICATIONS INTERNATIONAL, LTD.

ISBN:0-7853-1227-7

Library of Congress Catalog Card Number: 95-69018

Photography

The editors gratefully acknowledge the cooperation those who supplied photography to help make this book possible. They are listed below, along with the page number(s) on which their photos appear:

Ken Beebe: 26,27,28,29,38,39, back cover; **Scott Brandt:** 12,13; **Joe Bohovic:** 190,191; **Chan Bush:** 78,79,111; **Brandt Rosenbush, Chrysler Historical:** front cover, 40,41; **David Chobat:** 147; **Alex Gabbard:** 105,110,111; **Thomas Glatch:** 74,75,106,107,166,167; **Sam Griffith:** 8,9,20,21,24,25,62,63,88,89,98,99,126,127,198,199; **Jerry Heasley:** 84,85, 86,87,108,109,128,129,134,135,144,145,150,151,180,181,196,197,212,213; **Bud Juneau:** 60,61,92,93,96,97,120,121,122,123,186,187188,189; **Milton Gene Kieft:** 30,31; **Kugler Studio:** 64,65; **Phil Kunz:** 192,193,214,215; **Dan Lyons:** 32,33,202,203; **Vince Manocchi:** 58,59,70,71,168,169; **Jeff Medves:** 147; **Doug Mitchel:** 22,23,34,35,56,57,82,83,90, 91,116,117,142,143,146,162,163,172,173,182,183,210,211,back cover; **Mike Mueller:** 14,15,16,17,18,19,42,43,44,45,46,47,50,51,66,67,68,69,94,95,102,103,105,112,113,114, 115,118,119,130,131,132,133,152,153,160,161,170,171,204,205, back cover; ***Muscle Car Review*/Tom Shaw:** 10,11; **NHRA:** 6–7,41; **Rob Reaser:** 148,149; **Tom Salter:** 80,81,184,185; **Tom Shaw:** 158,159; **Rick Simmons:** 36,37; **Jim Smart:** 48,49,76,77,136; **Robert Sorgatz:** 100,101; **Richard Spiegelman:** 52,53,206,207; **Charley Thomas:** 137; **Nicky Wright:** 21,54,55,72,73,104,105,124,125,137,138,139,140,141,154,155,156,157, 164,165,174,175,176,177,178,179,208,209.

Owners

Special thanks to the owners of the cars featured in this book for their enthusiastic cooperation. They are listed below, along with the page number(s) on which their cars appear:

Kenneth J. Patt:8,9; **Robert & Karen Christanell:**12,13; **Phil Fair:**14,15; **Kenneth & Linda Coleman:**16,17; **Henry Hart:**18,19; **Bill Jackson:** 20,21; **Classic Car Centre:**21,174,175; **Guy Mabee:** 22,23; **Allan & Louise Gartzman:** 24,25; **Frank Spittle:** 26,27,28,29,38,39; **Dennis A. Urban:** 30,31; **Don McLennan:** 32,33; **Lynn Johnson:** 34, 35; **Steven Shuman:**36,37; **Marvin Friedman/Autoputer,Inc.:**44,45; **Dennis M. Phipps:** 46,47; **Glenn Cole:**52,53; **Jerry & Carol Buczkowski:**54,55,124,125; **James & Mary Engle:** 56,57; **Harry & Virgina Demenge:**58,59; **Chris Terry:**60,61; **Richard Witek:** 62,63; **Larry & Karen Miller:**64,65; **Paul McGuire:**68,69; **Bill Bush:**70,71; **Tom & Nancy Stump:**72,73; **Nate Studer:**74,75; **Roger Holdaway/"Car Stor:"** 78,79; **Classic Auto Showplace:**80,81; **Jeff & Trish Holmes:**82,83; **James Lojewski:**88,89; **Gerri Randolph:**90,91; **Ramshead Auto Collection:**92,93,96,97; **Dennis J. Guest:**98,99; **Jim Labertew:**100,101; **Gerald King:**104,105; **Samuel Pampenella Jr.:**105; **Doug & Judy Badgley:**106,107; **Dan Curry:**108,109; **Steve Maysonet:**114,115; **Rodney Brumbaugh:** 116,117; **Marion & Walter Gutowski:**118,119; **Charley Liddard:** 120,121,122,123; **Ed Cunneen:**126,127;**Roger Adkins:**128,129; **Scott Rosenthal:**137; **Steve Tucker:**137; **Al Fraser:**138,139; **Robert Fraser:**140,141; **Andrew Peterson:**142,143; **Tom Schlitter:** 144,145; **Ron Voyles:**146; **Glenn Moist:**147; **William Peterson:**147; **Bud Moore:**147; **Dick Knight:**148,149; **Robert & Ann Klein:**154,155; **Browney L. Mascow:**156,157; **Bruce Rhoades:**162,163; **Darryl A. Salisbury:**164,165; **Patrick Wnek:**166,167; **June Cecil:**168,169; **Barry Waddell:**170,171; **Jim & John Russell:**172,173; **Larry Bell:** 176,177; **Stephen Wither:**178,179; **Jim Reilly:**182,183; **Classic Auto Showplace:** 184,185; **Dave Cobble:**186,187; **Glen Stidger:**188,189; **Philip Lagerquist:**194,195; **Yoshio & Eric Nakayama:**198,199; **Barb Hillick:**200,201; **Paul D. Pierce:**202,203; **Don & Karen Kerridge:**208,209; **Danny & Steve Runyon:**212,213.

Contents

About the specifications in this book: The data describe as closely as possible the car pictured. Thus, the curb weight and price reflect the specific body style as equipped with the powertrain and options shown. The engine information is similarly keyed to the model displayed. Production figures show, where data is available, the number of models built with that body style and the specific engine described. Finally, the representative performance is the average of contemporary road tests.

Foreword

*Y*ou're running strong tonight. The big V-8's eager to rev, and the shifter feels good in your hand. You roll up to the traffic light. In the next lane is a gleaming blue coupe. Bulging hood, red-line tires, an anxious note to its exhaust. You take this in at a glance, but pretend not to. He does the same. Then he blips the throttle. And you know what's coming.

You don't usually do this. A pre-arranged run on an open road is more your style. That's where the serious work is done, sometimes for a little cash. And not from a dead stop. That's too hard on the drivetrain, and it attracts the wrong kind of attention. More likely you'll run side by side at 25 mph or so, then hammer it. The business is settled when one of you can no longer keep up.

But this guy in the next lane keeps goosing that gas pedal. You glance down the street. Traffic is sparse. The pavement is dry. Your peripheral vision catches the traffic light on the cross street as it flips to yellow. The orange needle on your tach begins its climb.

On green, he's gone. But you've nailed it, too. Wide ovals fight for traction, then hook up, and you both catapult ahead. A roar engulfs your car, peaking an instant before you crack off a full-throttle upshift. Your rear tires chirp, and the tail yaws, then snaps back. You've got a fender on him. Then a car length. You see the blue coupe's nose rise with his next gear change. But you're pulling away. Orbs of light from street lamps race up your hood, scatter over the windshield. You lift. He hangs back. In your mirror, his turn signal flashes. He slows and takes the next left. It's over. You both were a little lucky. But you were faster.

Muscle cars created their own culture, one with its own language, customs, and legends. And though the automakers made a big show of backing only sanctioned quarter-mile competition, and even embraced road racing and NASCAR action, it was Detroit's whispered secret and young America's unshakable knowledge that reputations were earned, and the pecking order established, on the street.

These were the cars that reigned over that reality. These were the Kings of the Street.

1960 Chrysler 300F

*I*n the formative years of factory performance, automakers re-served their hottest engines for their largest—and usually most-expensive—models.

Early Chrysler muscle was best expressed by the stylish and exclusive "letter-series" cars. First of these was the 1955 C-300 with its 300-bhp Hemi-head V-8. The 1960 300F continued the tradition of power and panache with its special trim and a sporty interior that boasted four bucket-type leather seats and a full-length console.

Chrysler specified its most-advanced engines for these image leaders. A dual-quad 413-cid wedge replaced the hemi in the '59 letter-series. It made the same 380 bhp as the previous year's standard 392-cid Hemi, but was 100 pounds lighter and simpler to build.

For '60, the 413 gained a radical ram induction system in which each four-barrel carb fed the opposite cylinder bank via 30-inch "outrigger" tubes. The length of the runners was calculated to produce a super-

charging effect in the heart of the rpm range.

Ram induction was available on 361- and 383-cid Dodge and Plymouth engines, but only Chryslers and Imperials could get the 413, and only the 300F had ram induction standard.

Horsepower was 375; optional "short-ram" tubes, which looked the same but differed internally, yielded 400 bhp at 5200 rpm and 465 lb-ft of torque at 3600. Pushbutton TorqueFlite automatic was standard, but a French-built four-speed manual was optional for just this season, ending up in only a few 300Fs.

Chrysler built 964 300F hardtops and 248 convertibles for '60, a peak year for letter-series performance. The 400-bhp option wasn't offered after the '62 300H, and thereafter the cars became less and less distinct from regular models until the true letter-series concluded with the '65 300L. These striking automobiles were a bridge from the days of sporty elegance to the age of Detroit muscle.

Specifications

1960 Chrysler 300F

Wheelbase, in. 126.0

Weight, lbs. 4270

Production 1212

Price $5411

Engine ohv V-8

Displacement, cid 413

Fuel system 2 × 4bbl.

Compression ratio 10.0:1

Horsepower @ rpm 375 @ 5000

Torque @ rpm 495 @ 2800

Representative performance

0-60 mph, sec. 7.0

¼ mile, sec. @ mph 16.00 @ 85.0

The vestigial spare tire harkened to an earlier age, but the 300F looked to the future with a high-tech, big-inch V-8 and capable road manners. Its dual-quad, cross-ram setup was a visual feast, while automatic-swiveling front seats, full-length console, and leather upholstery made for sophisticated accommodations. This was Chrysler's first year with weight-saving unibody construction.

1961 Chevrolet
Impala SS 409

*C*hevrolet brought real power to the people during 1961, and did so with style. The midyear introduction of the Super Sport option package showcased another new arrival, the 409-cid V-8.

A bargain at just $53.80, the SS "kit" was offered on any Impala. It included Super Sport trim inside and out, chassis reinforcements, stronger springs and shocks, power brakes with sintered metallic linings, spinner-type wheel covers, and one of Chevy's earliest uses of narrow-band whitewall tires. The dashboard gained a Corvette-type passenger grab bar and the steering column got a 7000-rpm tachometer.

Only Chevy's toughest V-8s were offered with the SS kit. The available 348-cid mills ranged from a four-barrel with 305 bhp to a tri-carb with 350. The other choice was the 409. Essentially a larger-displacement 348, its upgrades included forged aluminum pistons, a wilder camshaft, and 11.25:1 compression. A single four-barrel mated to the aluminum manifold. It made 360 bhp. It also made history.

Chevy built 491,000 Impalas for '61. Only 453 had the SS package and of those, just 142 got the 409. But word spread quickly. Here was a mainstream Chevy V-8 with 409 lb-ft of torque and the ability to turn mid-15-second quarter-miles with the standard 3.36:1 rear axle and mandatory four-speed manual. "She's real fine, my 409," sang the Beach Boys, and a legend was born.

The SS badge would grace great Chevys into the 1970s. The 409 lasted only through 1965. It would eventually make as much as 425 bhp and be offered even in stripper Bel Airs and Biscaynes. But a basic design traced to a late-1950s truck engine and incompatibility with serious performance hop-ups doomed it in an era of modern high-performance engines.

All told, the 409 went into just 43,775 cars. That its reputation outshines its production numbers shows how much impact the 409 had on muscle's early days.

Specifications

1961 Chevrolet Impala SS 409

Wheelbase, in. 119.0

Weight, lbs. 3700

Production 142

Price $2900

Engine ohv V-8

Displacement, cid 409

Fuel system 1 × 4bbl.

Compression ratio 11.25:1

Horsepower @ rpm 360 @ 5800

Torque @ rpm 409 @ 3600

Representative performance

0-60 mph, sec. 7.8

¼ mile, sec. @ mph 15.8 @ 94.1

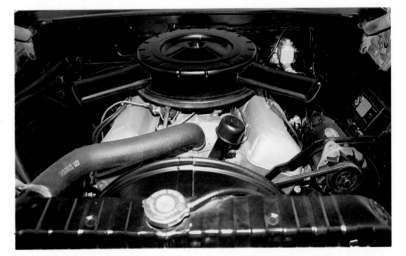

Mid 1961 saw the unveiling of two Chevrolet icons, the Super Sport package and the 409-cid V-8. Debuting on hardtop and convertible Impalas, the SS option initially included narrow whitewalls, SS tags, a passenger grab bar, a steering-column tachometer, and suspension upgrades. An instant legend, the 409 bowed with a four-barrel carb, 360 bhp, and mandatory four-speed. It would later get dual quads and up to 425 bhp.

1961 Pontiac Ventura 389

*P*ontiac enlarged its 370-cid V-8 in 1959 to create the 389, its signature engine for much of the '60s. A 345-bhp tri-power option was offered from the start and over the next few years, dealer-installed "Super Duty" factory mods pushed it to 363 bhp.

Introduction of the 389 coincided with the emergence of Ace Wilson's Royal Pontiac dealership in Royal Oak, Michigan, as the quasi-official street-performance arm of the factory. It specialized in the hottest factory parts and in super-tuning Ponchos. A four-speed 363-bhp Catalina prepped by Royal and driven by Pontiac marketing exec Jim Wangers was NHRA Super/Stock champ with an ET of 14.1 at 100 mph.

Pontiac downsized its midrange Catalina and Ventura for '61. Wheelbase dropped from 122 inches to 119, and bodies were shortened by four inches. Most customers winced; rodders cheered. The cars were 200 pounds lighter, and the 389 was strong as ever.

Pontiac now offered a wider array of serious performance equipment than any manufacturer, including aluminum front bumpers, radiators, and body parts. Late in the model year, Super Duty 389 hardware was applied to about a dozen 421-cid V-8s intended for pro drag racing.

Other race-ready big-blocks were available in small numbers at the time. But of cars within reach, few blended speed and style like a 389 Catalina or Ventura. Two-barrel versions had as much as 267 bhp, four-barrels had up to 333. The top box-stock choice was the 348-bhp tri-power.

Hardtops had GM's graceful "bubble-top" shape, Venturas came with "Jeweltone Morrokide" upholstery, and buyers could order a host of sporting accessories. A Borg-Warner four-speed manual was now a $306 production item, having previously been a special-order factory option. And Pontiac now authorized dealers to install genuine Hurst shifters for the three-speed manual.

Specifications

1961 Pontiac Ventura 389

Wheelbase, in. 119.0

Weight, lbs. 3685

Production NA

Price $3200

Engine ohv V-8

Displacement, cid 389

Fuel system 3 × 2bbl.

Compression ratio 10.75:1

Horsepower @ rpm 348 @ 4800

Torque @ rpm 430 @ 3200

Representative performance

0-60 mph, sec. 8.2

¼ mile, sec. @ mph 15.5 @ 93

Pontiac's trademark split-grille returned to stay for '61, while Bonneville luxury and Catalina svelteness came together in the Ventura Sport Coupe. The 389 was all business, with a mundane air cleaner hiding three two-barrel carbs. But the eight-lug wheel combined beauty and function. The wheel rim bolted to the outer portion of the aluminum brake drum, which doubled as the wheel hub and was finned to improve brake cooling. It was a $107 option. "Jeweltone Morrokide" upholstery was standard on Ventura.

1962 Dodge Dart 413

*I*ts time in the limelight was short, but the Max Wedge 413 was the engine that put Mopar in the muscle big leagues. The 413-cid V-8 had been around since 1959, but not until '61 did it find its way out of big Chryslers and into smaller Dodges and Plymouths.

There it made as much as 375 bhp, but with 400-bhp-plus Chevys, Pontiacs, and Fords afoot, Mopar needed more. All 413s had wedge-shaped combustion chambers, but the version unleashed in the spring of '62 was bred for maximum performance. That earned it the unofficial, but enduring, Max Wedge title.

Two versions were offered, both with solid lifters, aluminum pistons, Magnafluxed connecting rods, double-breaker ignition, twin 650-cfm Carter four-barrels, and beautiful three-inch headers that swept up along the side of the engine to clear the front suspension. The 11.0:1-compression Max Wedge had 410 bhp and 460 lb-ft of torque, the 13.5:1 variant made 420 bhp and 470 lb-ft.

Transmissions were a floor-shift three-speed manual or a fortified pushbutton TorqueFlite. Limited-slip 3.91:1 gears were standard, with ratios from 2.93:1 to 4.89:1 available. Sold as a package that included supporting hardware such as police-car suspension parts, prices for a Max Wedge ranged from $545 to $682, depending on the level of tune and transmission choice.

Heightening the impact of the Max Wedge's arrival was a revamp of the '62 Dodge and Plymouth lines. The full-size models—Dodge Dart and Polara, Plymouth Savoy, Belvedere, and Fury—dropped two inches in wheelbase and gained controversial new styling. The upside for performance buffs was a decrease in curb weight to near that of competitors' mid-size models, which had nothing to match the Max Wedge.

Turning mid-14s at over 100 mph box stock, a stripper $2900 Max Wedge Dart, said *Motor Trend,* "gives more performance per dollar than any other factory-assembled car in America."

Specifications
1962 Dodge Dart 413

Wheelbase, in. 116.0

Weight, lbs. 3260

Production NA

Price $3000

Engine ohv V-8

Displacement, cid 413

Fuel system 2 × 4bbl.

Compression ratio 11.0:1

Horsepower @ rpm 410 @ 5200

Torque @ rpm 460 @ 4400

Representative performance

0-60 mph, sec. 5.8

¼ mile, sec. @ mph 14.4 @ 101

Dart was the cheapest "big" Dodge, and was 200 pounds lighter than a Chevy Bel Air. "More live action because there's less dead weight," said Dodge. And how! A stock stripper like this carried just eight pounds per horsepower, but the skinny bias-ply tires were tormented coming off the line.

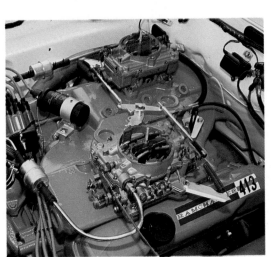

1962 Ford Galaxie 406

*F*ord began 1962 without an engine over 400 cid, a serious deficiency against 409 Chevys, 413 Mopars, and 421 Pontiacs. The remedy came part-way into the season with an enlargement of the 390-cid Ford to 406 cubic inches.

Called the Thunderbird 406 High-Performance-V-8, but available only in the Galaxie, the new engine cost $380 and came with a heavy-duty suspension, fade-resistant drum brakes, high-capacity radiator, and 15-inch wheels instead of 14s.

Breathing through a single Holley four-barrel, the 406 had 385 bhp at 5800 rpm and 440 lb-ft of torque at 3800. As the Super High-Performance Tri-Power, it put three Holley two-barrels under a lovely oval air cleaner and was rated at 405 bhp. Both versions had 11.4:1 compression and cast-in headers that led to low-restriction dual exhausts. Ford's Borg-Warner four-speed manual was mandatory and axle ratios as high as 4:11.1 could replace the standard 3.50:1 cog.

Most 406s went into Galaxie 500 hardtops and pillared coupes, but some were ordered in another midyear addition, the full-zoot 500XL hardtop coupe and 500XL Sunliner convertible.

A base 406 would scoot to 60 mph in 7.1 seconds; the tri-power was about a half-second quicker to 60. Quarter-mile times in the mid-15s were the rule with either version.

In sanctioned drag racing, the 406 Fords were still too heavy to out-run the top guns from Dodge, Plymouth, Chevy, and Pontiac. Ford shaved 164 pounds off the competition versions by offering aluminum bumpers and fiberglass body panels, but to no avail.

On the street, however, a rival who didn't notice the gold "406" emblem on the front fender could easily get caught napping by one of these newly fortified Galaxies. *Motor Trend* said the engine provided "something like Ferrari performance at a fifth of the price." The 406 was also made available in full-size Mercury models for late '62.

Ford General Manager Lee Iacocca pioneered the springtime product launch, and in mid-'62, he unveiled the top-line Galaxie 500XL series. The "500" denoted miles covered in the big NASCAR races. This Sunliner ragtop has optional stainless steel fender skirts, but bucket seats and console were standard. Its 406 is the tri-carb 405-bhp edition with the mandatory $188 four-speed.

1962 Pontiac Catalina
Super Duty 421

*T*he engine most identified with Pontiac's proud Super Duty label was the 421-cid V-8. Hand-built in a special factory tool room, the first Super Duty 421s debuted late in 1961 as race-only engines. Pontiac was vague on their output, but estimates ranged from 373 to 405 bhp. These were the largest-displacement mills offered at the time, and they helped spark Detroit's cubic-inch war.

NHRA rules changes for '62 required engines and body parts for the stock classes to be production pieces. This forced the 421 onto the official equipment sheet as an expensive, limited-run option. Fewer than 180 were built for '62, its peak production year. Most went into Catalinas, though 16 or so were installed in Pontiac's new personal-luxury coupe, the Grand Prix.

The '62 Super Duty 421 was officially rated at 405 bhp, but real output was closer to 460. Though street-legal, these again were race-ready engines, with four-bolt mains, forged rods and crank, solid lifters, and

NASCAR heads. Stock-car-racing versions used a single four-barrel, but street/strip Super Duty 421s had twin Carter 500-cfm four-barrels and an aluminum intake manifold. Free-flow cast-iron headers were fitted with easily removable exhaust dumps. Only three- and four-speed manuals were offered; Pontiac's automatic wasn't strong enough.

Reinforcing the division's hard-nosed performance attitude were a host of Super Duty options, including aluminum front-end body clips and a weight-cutting modified frame (the famous drilled "Swiss Cheese" frames wouldn't come until '63). These saved about 110 pounds. To shave another 40 pounds, the factory would fit aluminum exhaust manifolds. They were intended only for quarter-mile competition; Pontiac warned that subjected to more heat, the headers would melt.

Super Duty 421 Catalinas were fearsome on the street, and could dip into the 13s at more than 100 mph in the quarter—superior numbers for a regular-production car of the day.

Absence of chrome "Catalina" script on the front fenders helps identify this as one of the aluminum body-panel cars. Price of its dual-quad 421 engine alone was $2550, but included three-inch exhaust cutouts that could be unbolted to free up more power. The tri-tone upholstery looks great, but is incongruous in a car so competition oriented.

Specifications

1962 Pontiac Catalina Super Duty 421

Wheelbase, in. 120.0

Weight, lbs. 3575

Production 172

Price $5100

Engine ohv V-8

Displacement, cid 421

Fuel system 2 × 4bbl.

Compression ratio 11.0:1

Horsepower @ rpm 405 @ 5600

Torque @ rpm 425 @ 4400

Representative performance

0-60 mph, sec. 5.4

¼ mile, sec. @ mph 13.9 @ 107.0

1963 Ford Galaxie 427

"Total Performance" was Ford's slogan for '63, and midway through the model year, it delivered.

Galaxie 500 and 500XL hardtops got a new semi-fastback roofline good for an aerodynamic advantage on NASCAR superspeedways. At the same time, Ford introduced an enlarged version of its 390/406 V-8. The engine displaced 425 cubes, but playing off NASCAR's 427-cid limit, Ford called its new mill the 427.

A forged steel crankshaft and cross-bolted main bearing caps gave it strength. Forged aluminum pistons, a lightweight valvetrain, and a solid-lifter cam helped it survive at 7000 rpm. With two 652-cfm Holley four-barrels under an oval aluminum air cleaner, it made 425 bhp and 480 lb-ft of torque. With a single 780-cfm Holley, it made 410 bhp, and 476 lb-ft of torque. Both versions had 11.5:1 compression and an aluminum manifold.

Available on any full-size Ford, a 427 cost $406, or $462 for the dual-quad edition. Both came with a heavy-duty suspension, beefed-up drive-train and rear brakes, and 15-inch wheels instead of the 14s used on lesser Galaxies. A four-speed manual was a mandatory $188 option.

The "Sports Hardtops" were a hit in the showroom, and in stock-car racing they carried Ford to the '63 NASCAR title. Things were tougher on the drag strips, where Galaxies outweighed the competition by 300 pounds. Ford did field 50 race-only lightweights with fiberglass front clips, bare-metal interiors, and no sound deadening. A 3425-pound 'Glass Galaxie could turn low-12s at 118 mph in Super Stock, but even that wasn't good enough to win a single NHRA championship.

On backroads and boulevards, the 427 Galaxies held their own. But there were not nearly enough of them to remedy Ford's lackluster street reputation.

Specifications

1963 Ford Galaxie 500 427

Wheelbase, in. 119.0

Weight, lbs. 3700

Production NA

Price $3400

Engine ohv V-8

Displacement, cid 425

Fuel system 2 × 4bbl.

Compression ratio 11.5:1

Horsepower @ rpm 425 @ 6000

Torque @ rpm 480 @ 3700

Representative performance

0-60 mph, sec. 7.4

¼ mile, sec. @ mph 15.4 @ 95

Ford called its new semi-fastback the Sports Hardtop and its high-speed aero-dynamic advantage helped capture NASCAR's '63 manufacturer's title. It teamed with the hot new 425-cid V-8, which Ford billed as the "427." The 425-bhp version dressed to thrill with a lovely oval air cleaner over a pair of big Holley quads. Chrome valve covers were standard. The basic bench-seat interior of this Galaxie 500 reveals the optional four-speed that was mandatory with the 427 engine. Mercury also offered the 427s as the "Super Marauder" V-8s.

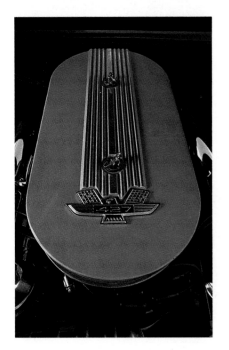

1963 Plymouth 426 Wedge

*D*odge's one-year flirtation with downsizing ended for 1963, and its big models returned to the 119-inch wheelbase. Plymouth stuck with the 116-inch span, but both divisions cleaned up the styling. No sign of fickleness under the hood, however, where the devastating new 426-cid wedge awaited.

This was basically a bored 413, again called the Ram Charger at Dodge and the Super Stock at Plymouth. Dual Carter four-barrels and the upswept ram's-head exhaust headers were retained. But the 426 got a host of internal beef-ups to make 415 bhp on 11.0:1 compression or 425 bhp on 13.5:1. Stage III 425-bhp versions followed during the year with further modifications including larger-bore carbs, recast heads, and 12.5:1 compression.

Preferred transmission was a heavy-duty TorqueFlite automatic, which again used pushbutton gear selection. The alternative was a floor-mounted three-speed manual; Chrysler didn't yet have a four-speed. Available axle ratios ranged from 2.93:1 to 4.89:1.

This was serious ordnance, ill-suited for everyday use. Indeed, brochures warned that the 426 was "not a street machine" but was "designed to be run in supervised, sanctioned drag-strip competition . . . Yet, it is stock in every sense of the word."

Plymouth offered the 426 wedge in all full-size models, from the sleeper Savoy to the luxury Sport Fury, and even made available a race-ready aluminum front-end package that trimmed 150 pounds.

Mopar's most-popular street performer in '63 was the 330-bhp 383-cid V-8. But the 426 wedge was there for the asking. *Hot Rod* fueled a 13.5:1-compression version with 102-octane and took it to the Pomona dragstrip. Running a TorqueFlite with a 4.56:1 gear, the magazine smoked a 12.69-second ET at 112 mph.

Full-size Dodges and Plymouths lost some of their eccentric styling for '63, but Belvederes like this one still gave little clue that 400-plus bhp was underhood. The interior was without frills. A floor-shifted three-speed manual or pushbutton TorqueFlite was used with the new 426 Wedge. This is the 415-bhp version. Hot Rod said Plymouth recommended that "full throttle bursts" with the 13.5:1-compression 425-bhp edition "be limited to 15 seconds." No problem. It could turn sub-13-second ETs.

1963 Pontiac Super Duty 421

Pontiac poured on so much performance for '63 that only an order from the highest power could slow it down. Unfortunately, that's what happened.

Super Duty 421s were back, tougher than ever. Compression jumped from 11.0:1 to 12.0:1, while other tweaks increased maximum shift points by 500 rpm, to a screaming 6400 rpm. The four-barrel version, set up for sustained high speeds, had 390 bhp. The dual-quad drag variant—now with aluminum exhaust manifolds standard and steel manifolds optional—was again underrated at 405 bhp. A second dual-quad drag rendition was introduced with a 13.0:1 squeeze. Pontiac timidly rated it at 410 bhp.

Factory weight-cutting again included aluminum front-end pieces and was joined by the famous Swiss Cheese frames, which had grapefruit-sized holes drilled into the chassis rails.

Super Duty 421s came only with a Hurst shifted three- or four-speed manual. Axle ratios up to 4.44:1 were offered. Dealers were advised to warn customers to maintain a minimum idle speed of 1000 rpm to insure adequate lubrication; that the engine would be cantankerous in cold weather, noisy all the time, and expensive to run; and that the large-capacity oil pan reduced ground clearance.

For those unwilling to take the Super Duty plunge, Pontiac introduced two new 421s that were more streetable. These High Output 421s had 10.75:1 compression and 353 bhp with a four-barrel or 370 bhp with three two-barrels.

Big Ponchos got new sheetmetal for '63, highlighted by trend-setting stacked headlamps. Pontiac was a force on the street and strip, while in NASCAR, it fought to retain its crown against the brutal new 427-cid Chevrolets.

It was all too much for GM. In January 1963, the corporation withdrew from organized racing and killed the Super Duty engines. Just 88 '63 Super Duty V-8s made it out the door, but Pontiac was poised to open a new performance frontier.

Stacked headlamps and fresh sheetmetal identified full-size '63 Pontiacs. Most of the Super Duty 421 engines, including this rare 405-bhp version, went into Catalinas. "CAUTION:" warned Pontiac's Special Equipment catalog, "This engine is designed specifically for maximum acceleration trials. Sustained speeds above 70 mph cannot be maintained without risking severe damage to the aluminum exhaust manifolds." The alloy manifolds saved 45 pounds. This four-speed Sports Coupe features the new factory option tachometer.

1964 Dodge 426 Hemi

At the center of Chrysler's contribution to American high performance is a storied engine of remarkable achievement: the Hemi. The company's original run of Hemi V-8s ended in 1958, with a 390-bhp 392-cid edition. The design was sound—large, hemispherical combustion chambers are highly efficient—but Hemis were complex, heavy, and expensive.

By the early 1960s, stakes were high enough for Chrysler to try again. To win on NASCAR's new superspeedways, and to dominate at the cutting-edge of drag racing, Mopar engineers developed a Hemi based on the 413/426 wedge-head engines. It still was costly and complicated, but the new mill weighed just 67 pounds more than the wedges. Maximum advertised horsepower for the 426-cid Hemi was 425. Rumor had dyno needles breaking at 600 bhp.

These engines were reserved for racing, and their impact was immediate. Debuting at the Daytona 500 in February 1964, they promptly swept the first three places in NASCAR's premier event. Stock-car racing Hemis had a single Holley four-barrel atop a dual-plane high-rise intake manifold and were used with a four-speed manual gearbox. Drag-racing versions had a ram-tuned aluminum induction system with Carter ABF dual quads. Available only in special-order intermediate-sized Dodge and Plymouth models, they ran the four-speed or the TorqueFlite automatic, which was in its last year with pushbuttons.

Available from the factory were a series of sub-12-second supercars that used aluminum for the hood, front fenders, doors, and some body panels. A lightened front bumper and magnesium front wheels were standard. The cars had no radio, no heater, no back seat or carpet, no sound deadening material. Feather-weight Dodge van bucket seats were used, the side windows were plastic, and the battery rode in the trunk.

Street versions of the Hemi engine wouldn't be available for a couple of years. But King Kong had arrived.

Specifications

1964 Dodge 426 Hemi

Wheelbase, in. 119.0

Weight, lbs. 3210

Production NA

Price $4600

Engine ohv V-8

Displacement, cid 426

Fuel system 2 × 4bbl.

Compression ratio 12.5:1

Horsepower @ rpm 425 @ 6000

Torque @ rpm 480 @ 4600

Representative performance

0-60 mph, sec. 4.1

¼ mile, sec. @ mph 11.40 @ 125

Arriving in 1964, the 426 Hemi immediately propelled Dodge and Plymouth into NASCAR's winner's circle and into drag-racing dominance. The most-popular Hemi Dodge was the mid-size 330/440/Polara. This is a 330 with the Maximum Performance Package. It's a factory-built, Super Stock-class quarter-miler with aluminum body panels and lightweight interior components. The race-Hemi powertrain uses a TorqueFlite with dash-mounted pushbuttons. It wouldn't have been pleasant, but this car was street-legal.

1964 Ford Thunderbolt

*E*ven with their strong 427-cid V-8s and lightened front ends, big body-on-frame Ford Galaxies were no match for the lighter-still unibody Dodges and Plymouths. The obvious solution was to stuff the 427 into the mid-size Fairlane. Nothing good comes easy.

With help from Dearborn Steel Tubing, a contract car builder, Ford concocted the race-ready and street-legal, if not exactly streetable, Thunderbolt.

Extensive front-end modifications were necessary to custom-fit the big-block, and eight equal-length exhaust headers had to be snaked through the suspension components. The competition 427's high-rise manifold elevated the air cleaner above the fenderline, requiring a teardrop-shaped hood bubble. It gulped air via screened inner headlight bezels. Transmissions were a Hurst-shifted four-speed with 4.44:1 gears or an automatic with 4.58:1. Massive traction bars, asymmetrical rear springs, and a trunk-mounted 95-pound bus battery helped get down what was realistically 500 bhp.

Weightcutting was merciless: plexiglass windows, and fiberglass front body panels, bumpers, and doors. Sunvisors, mirror, sound-deadener, armrests—even jack and lug wrench—were shed. The back seat stayed, but the fronts were lightweight police-package buckets.

At 3225 pounds, the T-bolt weighed more than a stock Fairlane. But it was only 20 pounds over its NHRA-class minimum. At last, Ford had a winner. ETs in the 11s earned Thunderbolt the Top Stock crown and Ford the '64 NHRA Manufacturer's Cup.

Anyone with $3780 ($200 more for automatic) could walk into a Ford dealer and order a Thunderbolt. Still, just one was assembled in 1963, 100 were built in '64, and two were built in '65. These were real race cars, and few went to battle on the public highways. As *Hot Rod* warned, the T-bolt was "not suitable for driving to and from the strip, let alone on the street in everyday use."

To compete in Super Stock drag racing against lighter rivals, Ford squeezed its competition 427 V-8 into the mid-size Fairlane and created the Thunderbolt. Fiberglass panels and an ultra-stark cabin kept its weight down. A trunk-mounted battery helped offset the 427's heft, while headlamp bezels transformed into air intakes fed the engine via huge underhood hoses. The teardrop hood bubble became a popular street-warrior accessory.

Specifications
1964 Ford Thunderbolt

Wheelbase, in. 115.5

Weight, lbs. 3225

Production 100

Price $3780

Engine ohv V-8

Displacement, cid 427

Fuel system 2 × 4bbl.

Compression ratio 12.7:1

Horsepower @ rpm 425 @ 6000

Torque @ rpm 480 @ 3700

Representative performance

0-60 mph, sec. NA

¼ mile, sec. @ mph 11.76 @ 122.7

1964 Oldsmobile Cutlass 4-4-2

A case can be made that the very first muscle car was the 1949 Oldsmobile Rocket 88, created when Olds shoehorned its 135-bhp big-car V-8 into a mid-size model. When Pontiac rejuvenated the concept with its 1964 Tempest GTO, Olds was compelled to respond.

It took until midyear, at which time Olds extended its Police Apprehender Pursuit package to its new intermediate-sized F-85/Cutlass series, which shared the Tempest/LeMans chassis.

The package used the top engine available in these Oldsmobiles, a 290-bhp 330-cid V-8, then added a high-lift cam, dual-snorkel air cleaner, and some other minor tweaks to come up with 310 bhp. The engine's four-barrel carb, in combination with the package's Chevy-built Muncie four-speed manual and the car's dual exhausts, gave the new option its name, 4-4-2.

Offered on any body style except the station wagon, the 4-4-2 package added $285 to an F-85 or $136 to the uplevel Cutlass. It included a heavy-duty suspension with anti-roll bars front and rear, plus "tiger paw" tires. Balanced manners were a goal from the start and some road testers called this new Oldsmobile the best-handling mid-size car in the GM stable.

With the standard 2.54:1 axle ratio, a Cutlass 4-4-2 turned a respectable 15.6-second quarter-mile at 89 mph for *Car Life*. By comparison, a 290-bhp Cutlass was two seconds slower to 60 mph and 1.3 seconds slower in the quarter-mile.

But where Pontiac successfully pitched its GTO to the youth market as a factory hot rod, Olds was more tentative in promoting its new muscle car; one of the few advertisements pictured a couple of cops in a four-door F-85 sedan that didn't even wear the tri-color 4-4-2 badge. Performance buffs just weren't used to looking at Olds, and only 2999 4-4-2s were sold this first season. Pontiac, by contrast, moved more than 32,000 GTOs in '64.

Specifications

1964 Oldsmobile Cutlass 4-4-2

Wheelbase, in. 115.0

Weight, lbs. 3770

Production 2999

Price $3500

Engine ohv V-8

Displacement, cid 330

Fuel system 1 × 4bbl.

Compression ratio 10.25:1

Horsepower @ rpm 310 @ 5200

Torque @ rpm 355 @ 3600

Representative performance

0-60 mph, sec. 7.4

¼ mile, sec. @ mph 15.6 @ 89

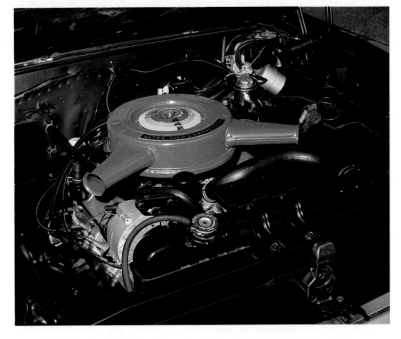

Olds could claim the first "muscle car" with the 1949 Rocket 88, but it didn't return to the formula until mid 1964 with an option package for the F-85/Cutlass series. Called the 4-4-2, it stood for four-barrel carb, four-speed manual, and dual exhausts. The car was no street eliminator, but a lightweight 330-cid V-8 and a well-tuned suspension made the 4-4-2 the best-handling American sedan of '64.

1964 Plymouth 426 Street Wedge

*D*espite warnings in 1963 that its raucous 426 Wedge engines were for competition-use only, Mopar found itself with plenty of unhappy buyers who bought it for street duty. For '64, Chrysler gave them a version of this engine specifically designed for everyday use and tagged it, appropriately enough, the Street Wedge.

Like the race-bred 415/425-bhp 426 Max Wedge, the Street Wedge was offered in Dodge's big models, which had a 119-inch wheelbase, and in the full-size Plymouth Savoy/Belvedere/Fury range, which retained the 116-inch wheelbase. Revised grilles and a new, reverse-tapering rear roof pillar freshened the '64 models.

Unlike the Max Wedge, this new 426 had such features as a provision to heat the manifold so that it would start in cold weather, and a 10.3:1 compression so it could run on something less than aviation fuel. Instead of dual quads, it had a single four-barrel on a conventional cast-iron intake manifold, and traditional exhaust headers instead of the

flamboyant ram's-head design of its predecessor.

It may have been detuned, but the Street Wedge wasn't defanged. High performance valve springs, pistons, plugs, and a hot cam were inside. Hydraulic lifters, dual breaker distributor, nonsilenced air cleaner, dual exhausts with cutouts, and heavy-duty brakes and suspension were part of the $483 "426-S" high-performance package. Horsepower was rated at 365, with a robust 470 lb-ft of torque at a low 3200 rpm.

Buyers could choose from a new Chrysler-built four-speed manual with Hurst linkage or the proven TorqueFlite three-speed automatic. A 3.23:1 axle was standard, but four-speed cars could get 2.93:1 or 3.55:1.

Motor Trend tested a Street Wedge Sport Fury hardtop, finding a combination of genuine muscle and liveable manners. The brakes were excellent, the suspension capable, and the rear axle well-behaved in drag-strip starts. "All in all," it concluded, "it's as good as they come in overall performance...."

Specifications

1964 Plymouth Sporty Fury 426 Street Wedge

Wheelbase, in. 116.0

Weight, lbs. 3720

Production NA

Price $3880

Engine ohv V-8

Displacement, cid 426

Fuel system 1 × 4bbl.

Compression ratio 10.3:1

Horsepower @ rpm 365 @ 4800

Torque @ rpm 475 @ 3200

Representative performance

0-60 mph, sec. 6.8

¼ mile, sec. @ mph 15.2 @ 95.5

Mopar's answer for those who wanted something a little tamer than the rowdy race-bred 426-cid Wedge V-8 was a new, less-radical version called the Street Wedge. It was an option in full-size models, including Plymouth's top-of-the-line Sport Fury hardtop, which got new tapered rear roof pillars. The handsome vinyl-bucket seat interior featured a floor shifter for the optional automatic (pushbuttons were discontinued after '63). Fury's console-mounted tachometer was a $50 extra and its location made it hard to read from the driver's seat.

1964 Pontiac Tempest GTO

*T*he Big Bang in modern muscle's evolution is the 1964 GTO. This is where it began: a mid-size automobile with a big, high-power V-8 marketed as an integrated high-performance package—the very definition of the muscle car.

To create the GTO, Pontiac sidestepped GM's prohibition on intermediate-sized cars having engines over 330 cid. In a ploy that didn't require corporate approval, Pontiac made its 389-cid V-8 part of a $296 option package for the new Tempest. The name *Gran Turismo Omologato* was boldly appropriated from the Ferrari GTO. Roughly translated, it means a production grand touring machine sanctioned for competition.

Pontiac hoped to sell 5000 '64 GTOs; it sold 32,450. The Goat, as it was affectionately dubbed, generated a cult following and sent rivals scrambling to come up with similar machines.

To create an engine worthy of its original, Pontiac fortified the 389

with a high-lift cam and the 421-cid V-8's high-output heads. The GTO had 325 bhp with the standard Carter four-barrel. About 8250 of the cars were ordered with the extra-cost Tri-Power setup—three Rochester two-barrels—and were rated at 348 bhp. Both versions had 10.75:1 compression and 428 lb-ft of torque. The standard three-speed manual and optional four-speed used Hurst linkages; a two-speed automatic also was optional.

A thick front sway bar, heavy-duty shocks, stiffened springs, and high-speed 14-inch tires were included. A $75 "roadability group" added sintered metallic brake linings and a limited-slip diff. The sporting attitude carried over inside, where all GTOs got bucket seats and an engine-turned aluminum instrument surround.

Four-barrel Goats typically ran 0-60 mph in about 7.5 seconds and the quarter in 15.7 at 92 mph. Tri-Power GTOs were consistently quicker and added immeasurably to the car's mystique.

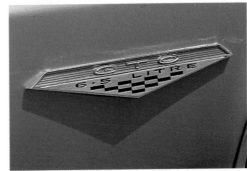

Specifications

1964 Pontiac Tempest GTO

Wheelbase, in. 115.0

Weight, lbs. 3470

Production 32,450

Price $2852

Engine ohv V-8

Displacement, cid 389

Fuel system 3 × 2bbl.

Compression ratio 10.75:1

Horsepower @ rpm 348 @ 4900

Torque @ rpm 428 @ 3600

Representative performance

0-60 mph, sec. 6.6

¼ mile, sec. @ mph 14.8 @ 95

Pontiac created the first modern muscle car by putting a big V-8 into the midsize Tempest/LeMans body. A convertible, hardtop, and this pillared coupe were offered. The 389-cid mill used a four-barrel carb or this hot triple two-barrel setup. Bucket seats were standard. Woodgrain steering wheel, center console, Hurst-shifted four-speed manual, and simulated wire wheel covers are among this Goat's factory options.

1965 Buick Skylark Gran Sport

*G*eneral Motors bowed to the performance tide in 1965, authorizing engines up to 400 cid in its intermediate cars. Buick seized the change as a chance to put some spark in the Skylark.

The division's big-block V-8 actually displaced 401 cubic inches. Undeterred, Buick simply renamed it the "400," slipped it into its mid-size model, and created the Gran Sport. Teamed with a heavy-duty radiator and dual-exhausts, the 401 carried the same 325-bhp rating as in Buick's full-size models. ("Wildcat 445" on the air cleaner referred to the engine's torque rating.)

To Buick's credit, the operation was more than just an engine transplant. Any Gran Sport—hardtop, pillared coupe, or convertible—got the convertible's beefed-up frame for better rigidity, plus specially valved shocks and heavy-duty springs. Up front went a thick anti-roll bar. The rear suspension got added links to fight axle windup and differential

twist. Braking was improved with enlarged front-wheel cylinders.

With the standard three-speed manual, the Gran Sport package added $253 to the cost of a regular Skylark. It jumped to $420 with the four-speed manual, and to $457 with Buick's two-speed Super Turbine 300 automatic. Top available axle ratio was 3.73:1. All Gran Sports had to be ordered with bucket seats, a $72 "mandatory option." Positraction should have been madatory, too. As with other high-powered intermediates, wheel spin off the line was a problem.

But buyers were happy. This was a solid car with a smooth, responsive engine, good ride quality, and competent handling. *Motor Trend* remarked that its 12.3 mpg in city driving was "not bad at all." Buick sold nearly 70,000 Gran Sports that first year, and no one seemed to mind that it wasn't an all-out muscle car. That would come soon enough.

A Skylark with the Gran Sport option created Buick's first muscle car. Its 401-cid V-8 was advertised as a 400-cid engine—and referred to on the air cleaner as the "Wildcat 445" in recognition of its torque output. This one has automatic transmission, but not the extra-cost tachometer that would have occupied the pod at the console's forward edge.

1965 Chevrolet
Chevelle SS 396

*C*hevelle's climb to muscle-car stardom began with a couple of mid-1965 maneuvers to recapture lost ground. Chevelle had entered its second year with some minor appearance changes inside and out, but Chevrolet again found itself chasing Pontiac, Oldsmobile, and even Buick in midsize performance.

While the GTO, 4-4-2, and Skylark Gran Sport had large-displacement V-8s for '65, Chevelle stayed loyal to small-block power. No apologies were needed for Chevy's excellent 327, especially in new 350-bhp tune. Available at midyear, the L79 327 was essentially a hydraulic-lifter version of Corvette's 365-bhp 327. With the mandatory four-speed and a Positraction 3.31:1 rear axle, an L79 Malibu Super Sport could turn quarter-miles in the high 14s.

But the bow tie guys had seen the future, and it was genuine big-cube go in an intermediate-sized package. Their reaction was another midyear addition, this one a limited-edition option that found its way into just 200

Malibu SS hardtops and one convertible. Tagged the Z-16 package, it retailed for $1501 and was built around a hot 375-bhp 396-cid V-8.

Again, this Turbo-Jet 396 was basically a hydraulic-lifter variant of the 425-bhp 396 available in the Corvette. But in creating the Malibu SS 396, Chevy strengthened the Chevelle with a stouter convertible-type frame, a beefed-up front suspension, anti-roll bars front and rear, bigger brakes, and faster power-assisted steering. A Muncie four-speed was mandatory, with axle ratios as high as 4.56:1 available as an alternative to the standard 3.31:1 gears. Rounding out the Z-16 package was a 160-mph speedometer, a 6000-rpm tach, and an AM/FM stereo radio.

With 58 percent of its weight over the front axle, a Malibu SS 396 floundered through corners, but its mid-14-second quarter-mile times at around 100 mph were very strong for 1965. Super Sport production peaked this year, accounting for 101,577 of the 326,977 Chevelles built. None was rarer or more rapid than the Z-16.

Specifications

1965 Chevrolet Chevelle Malibu SS 396 Z-16

Wheelbase, in. 115.0

Weight, lbs. 3600

Production 201

Price $4100

Engine ohv V-8

Displacement, cid 396

Fuel system 1 × 4bbl.

Compression ratio 11.0:1

Horsepower @ rpm 375 @ 5600

Torque @ rpm 420 @ 3600

Representative performance

0-60 mph, sec. 6.0

¼ mile, sec. @ mph 14.66 @ 99.8

Chevelle muscled its way into big-cube performance in '65 with the Z-16 package. The $1501 limited-edition option used a 375-bhp Corvette V-8 to create the first SS 396. Bucket seats and console were standard; the simulated wood steering wheel was an option, and the dash-top tach a mandatory extra.

1965 Dodge/Plymouth
Factory Altered Wheelbase

With proper exhaust systems, there was no reason Chrysler's 1965 Factory Altered Wheelbase cars wouldn't have been street-legal. Clearly, though, they were intended for competition and their target was the premier showcase for the hottest manufacturer equipment: the NHRA's Factory Experimental class. FX was a zone beyond Super Stock. Super Stockers were models sold to the public. FX cars need only use factory optional equipment—they need not be showroom available.

Hemi engines and lightweight body parts already were optional in midsize Mopars. The next frontier was weight transfer to optimize traction off the line. Chrysler's solution was to design six Dodge Coronets and six Plymouth Belvederes that put maximum weight on the back axles. The front and rear wheels were moved far forward of their stock position and the wheelbase itself was shortened by 5.5 percent.

Viewing the first of these cars prior to the '65 season, NHRA inspectors recoiled. Chrysler had gone too far. A wheelbase-alteration limit of two percent was quickly instituted, effectively banning the new Mopars from NHRA FX competition. It didn't much matter. The Dodge and Plymouth factory drag teams did an end run around the NHRA. The cars became a sensation running as AHRA Factory Experimentals and in lucrative exhibition matches nationwide. Capacity crowds turned out to see such popular drivers as Dick Landy, Butch Leal, Dave Strickler, and Ronnie Sox at the wheel.

The Factory Altered Wheelbase Mopars were the ultimate production-based muscle cars, and were in effect missing links between the Super Stock factory lightweights of the early '60s and the all-out Funny Cars that were just over the horizon.

The 426 Hemi was a "production" engine, but was still race-intended in '65. It had about 550 bhp with dual quads. After being outlawed by the NHRA, Altered Wheelbase racers used a Chrysler-engineered Hilborn fuel-injection system with 14-inch velocity stacks that gave their Hemis over 600 bhp.

Fiberglass body panels were technically factory options for midsize Mopars in 1965. The complete set shown here cost $410 and weighed just 80 pounds. On Altered Wheelbase cars, the panels mated to acid-dipped steel unibodies to create racers that tipped the scales at 3050 pounds, including fuel and fluids.

Traction off the line was superior thanks to excellent weight transfer. Typical ETs were 10.20 seconds at 138 mph with the dual-quad Hemi and in the low- to mid-9s at 143 mph with the later fuel-injected versions.

Racer "Bud" Faubel in an Altered Wheelbase Coronet shown as it came from the factory. The axles were moved forward—the rear one by 15 inches, the front by 10—to create a 110-inch wheelbase racer that put about 56 percent of the car's weight over the rear tires. Note the stock appearance of the dashboard.

1965 Oldsmobile Cutlass 4-4-2

*O*ldsmobile took the hint. Shuffling onto the burgeoning performance scene in mid 1964 with a "police package" that could be ordered on a four-door sedan was no recipe for muscle-car success. Indeed, fewer than 3000 buyers bought the original 4-4-2.

Refining its strategy for '65, Olds made the 4-4-2 a $190 option only on the F-85 pillared coupe, and a $156 extra on the Cutlass coupe, two-door hardtop, and convertible. Styling of these mid-size models was updated, with the 4-4-2 distinguished by chrome bodyside tines.

Marketing was hipper, too. Instead of a couple of cops in a bland '64 sedan, 4-4-2 advertising for '65 burst with references to cubic inches and horsepower. Buzzwords like "kicks" and "cool" flew freely. One spot showed nothing but blurred asphalt and the declaration, "Olds 4-4-2 was here!"

GM itself got the message and raised the displacement ceiling on intermediates to 400 cubic inches. Olds destroked and debored its new 425-cid big-car V-8 to create a hot 400-cid V-8 exclusively for the

4-4-2. Now the name meant 400 cubes, four-barrel carb, and dual exhausts.

Horsepower increased by 35, to 345, and torque expanded by 85 lb-ft, to 440. Peak power now came at 4800 rpm, not 5200, and peak torque was on tap at just 3200 rpm, 400 rpm lower than before.

Olds was able to use a mild cam and relatively modest axle ratios to fashion a mannered muscle car that still went quite well. Careful suspension tuning and anti-roll bars front and rear again helped it handle better than the other GM intermediates. Transmission choices were three- and four-speed manuals and the two-speed Jetaway automatic.

Where the 4-4-2 stayed too conservative was inside: Instrumentation was run-of-the-mill F-85 with a tachometer mounted too low to be of much use. But its effortless performance proved prophetic.

"It oozes out 345 bhp without trying," noticed *Car Life* in May 1965, "hinting of things to come if this big engine/little car kick lasts."

Specifications

1965 Oldsmobile Cutlass 4-4-2

Wheelbase, in. 115.0

Weight, lbs. 3890

Production NA

Price $3370

Engine ohv V-8

Displacement, cid 400

Fuel system 1 × 4bbl.

Compression ratio 10.25:1

Horsepower @ rpm 345 @ 4800

Torque @ rpm 440 @ 3200

Representative performance

0-60 mph, sec. 5.5

¼ mile, sec. @ mph 15.0 @ 98

With introduction of a new and larger V-8, 4-4-2 now stood for 400 cubic inches, four-barrel carb, and dual exhausts. Overall balance continued to be its forte. "It's good and fast, and its handling and general road behavior are better than ninety percent of the cars bought by American car consumers," said Car and Driver.

1965 Pontiac
Tempest GTO

*B*y its second season, the GTO was being celebrated in pop songs ("... three deuces and a four speed, and you're ready to roll ...") and coveted in showrooms (sales were doubling). There even were GTO shoes. Pontiac's tiger had its claws in the culture of young America.

Returning were hardtop and pillared coupes, and the ragtop, all with fresh front and rear styling: Grilles were recessed, headlamps were now stacked, and the hood gained a decorative scoop.

The 389-cid V-8 remained the only engine, but improvements in breathing and cam design boosted power. The base four-barrel increased by 10 bhp, to 335, and the Tri-Power gained 12, to 360. In August, Pontiac released an over-the-counter option kit for Tri-Power engines that opened the hood scoop and created the Goat's first ram-air setup.

Four-barrel cars came with 3.23:1 gears, Tri-Powers with 3.55:1; in all, six ratios, from 3.08:1 to 4.33:1, were available from the factory. A three-speed manual was standard and close- or wide-ratio four-speeds were optional; all had Hurst shifters. A two-speed automatic also was offered.

Inside, the GTO again set the pace for sporty cars. Bucket seats remained standard and the turned-alloy look of the gauge surround changed to woodgrain, with real wood used on some cars. New options included an $86 Rally cluster with full instrumentation and a $137 AM/FM radio. Also available were new Kelsey Hayes stamped steel Rally wheels with functional cooling slots.

Technically, the GTO was still a $296 Tempest option. Tri-power cost $116 extra and was ordered on 20,547 of the 75,352 GTOs built for '65. The car's encompassing approach to performance and style already was inspiring imitators. Many of them would go on to surpass the Goat in power and speed, but few would have made it off the drawing board if not for the winning ways of Pontiac's original.

Specifications

1965 Pontiac Tempest GTO

Wheelbase, in. 115.0

Weight, lbs. 3563

Production 20,547

Price $3200

Engine ohv V-8

Displacement, cid 389

Fuel system 3 × 2bbl.

Compression ratio 10.75:1

Horsepower @ rpm 360 @ 5200

Torque @ rpm 424 @ 3600

Representative performance

0-60 mph, sec. 6.1

¼ mile, sec. @ mph 14.7 @ 99

Though still technically an option for Tempest hardtops, pillared coupes, and convertibles, the GTO had already forged its own identity as America's premier performance car. This rag-top, one of 11,311 built for '65, has the Tri-Power setup. An over-the-counter option rendered the hood scoop functional for the first time. No muscle car had a sportier dashboard.

1966 Buick
Skylark Gran Sport

*B*uick's Skylark got fresh sheetmetal for '66, and there was more available power for the Gran Sport. But competition was tougher than ever, and sales of this upscale muscle car skidded dramatically in its second season.

Highlighting the new look were sloping sail panels that extended the rear roofline beyond the back window. Distinguishing the Gran Sport were a blacked-out grille, new GS emblems, nonfunctional rear-facing hood scoops, and simulated front-fender vents.

The base 401-cid "Wildcat 445" four-barrel again had 325 bhp, but a hotter 340-bhp version was made available during the model year. Dual exhausts and heavy-duty suspension were included as standard equipment with either engine. Metallic brake linings and a rear stabilizer bar were among the options.

A three-speed manual came with either version of the 401; a four-speed added $184, and SuperTurbine automatic cost $205. Half-a-dozen

axle ratios, from 2.78:1 to 4.30:1 were now offered, and a Positive Traction diff was a mandatory option with the performance cogs. Handsome $74 chrome-plated wheels were popular options, as were power steering ($95) and power brakes ($42). Buick would even delete the heater for a $71 credit.

The 340-bhp engine was tuned to run, redlining at 4600 rpm and making a peak 445 lb-ft of torque at 3200. It was nearly a second quicker to 60 mph than the base engine, and about a half-second faster in the quarter-mile. With the 3.36:1 axle, a 340-bhp GS got to 60 mph in 6.8 seconds and turned 14.9-second ETs at 95 mph.

It wasn't the fastest big-cube intermediate, but reviewers again lauded the Gran Sport's balanced nature. At $2956 for the pillared coupe, $3019 for the Sport Coupe, and $3167 for the convertible, however, base prices were higher than those of 4-4-2s and GTOs. Buick built 106,217 Skylarks for '66; just 13,816 of them were Gran Sports.

Specifications

1966 Buick Skylark Gran Sport

Wheelbase, in. 115.0

Weight, lbs. 3660

Production 13,816

Price $3558

Engine ohv V-8

Displacement, cid 401

Fuel system 1 × 4bbl.

Compression ratio 10.25:1

Horsepower @ rpm 325 @ 4400

Torque @ rpm 445 @ 2800

Representative performance

0-60 mph, sec. 7.6

¼ mile, sec. @ mph 15.47 @ 90.5

Despite the midyear addition of a 340-bhp version, the Gran Sport was oriented toward civilized performance, not bare-knuckles street fighting. New styling was graceful outside, but stodgy inside, despite excellent seating and the availability of a four-speed manual. Buick's "...Gran Sport has tremendous potential," said Car and Driver. *"If they ever decide to go to work, look out."*

1966 Chevrolet Biscayne 427

*H*ad it really been that long since 1962?

When the muscle era dawned, the turf was controlled by the likes of 409s, 413s, and Super Duty 421s in Detroit's mainline cruisers. But the performance world changed overnight in 1964. Tri-power GTOs, 427 Fairlane Thunderbolts, and the first sightings of the pony car established a new pecking order whose primacy was based on going the fastest with the least amount of car. The arrival of the Street Hemi in the 1966 Plymouth and Dodge midsize models made the revolution complete.

Still, the rise of each new age is accompanied by the embers of the one it replaces, and it was into such a time that the 427-powered Chevrolets were born.

A bored-out variation of the then year-old 396-cid V-8, the Turbo-Jet 427 debuted in 1966 Corvettes and full-size Chevys. Any member of the big-car line could be had with one of two versions: a hydraulic-lifter example with a 10.25:1 compression ratio and 390 bhp, or a solid-lifter variant with an 11.0:1 squeeze and 425 horses.

Chevy installed 15,517 427s in '66, the lion's share in Corvettes. Of the 5143 that went into big cars, 1856 were the 425-bhp L72. This was the engine of choice for those who believed speed was the only luxury worth having.

Those willing to forego the niceties of the more-upscale members of the facelifted '66 Chevy clan could spend just under $2500 for a bottom-of-the-line Biscayne two-door sedan. Another $232 fetched the Muncie M21 four-speed gearbox, and an additional $448 bought the L72 with its four-bolt main block, aluminum intake manifold, 780-cfm Holley four-barrel carburetor, enlarged intake valves, and big rectangular ports. A $32 F41 suspension option stiffened the springs, shocks, and front sway bar, and added a rear stabilizer bar and wider wheels.

By virtue of the two-door's relatively light weight, 427 Biscaynes were naturals for the NHRA's B/Stock class. Indeed, Wiley Cossey drove a similar 427 Bel Air to Junior Stock Eliminator honors at the 1966 Winternationals. The good old days were back, if even for just a little while.

Specifications

1966 Chevrolet Biscayne 427

Wheelbase, in. 119.0

Weight, lbs. 3500

Production NA

Price $3100

Engine ohv V-8

Displacement, cid 427

Fuel system 1 × 4bbl.

Compression ratio 11.0:1

Horsepower @ rpm 425 @ 5600

Torque @ rpm 460 @ 4000

Representative performance

0-60 mph, sec. 5.7

¼ mile, sec. @ mph 14.0 @ 102

Midsize muscle was all the rage by '66, but for those who still had a full-size appetite, Chevy was there. A Biscayne pillared coupe had milquetoast looks but mad-bull manners when ordered with the solid-lifter 425-bhp 427-cid L72 V-8. Taxicab hubcaps, four-speed manual, and no-frills bench-seat accommodations were requisite street-sleeper trappings.

1966 Chevrolet
Chevelle SS 396

*C*hevy repositioned its Super Sport Chevelle as an all-out performance car for '66, but in some ways, more turned out to be less.

Like other GM intermediates, it was reskinned, though dimensions hardly changed. SS models got a blackout grille and a new hood with nonfunctional vents. With engines of around 400 cid now obligatory in this game, Chevy made the 396-cid V-8 standard, so all its mid-size muscle cars were now Chevelle SS 396s.

But instead of the 375-bhp Z-16 396 that bowed midway through the '65 model year, the '66s got detuned 396s rated at 325 bhp in base Turbo-Jet guise and 360 bhp in optional L34 form. Both new mills had 10.25:1 compression, but the L34 got a taller cam, stronger block, and larger four-barrel. It cost $105 extra and nearly one-third of SS 396 buyers ordered it. Still, the L34's mid 15s at around 90 mph in the quarter were pretty ordinary.

So was much of the rest of the car, at least compared to the pricey,

limited-edition Z-16. Instead of reinforced brakes and underpinnings, the '66 SS 396 used standard Chevelle brakes and suspension pieces. Chevy claimed it had stiffer springs and shocks—an assertion some testers disputed once they experienced the car's wayward handling and subpar stopping ability. In fairness, comfortable seats, tractable engines, sporty styling, and a $2776 base price made the '66 SS 396 a great daily driver.

Then, in the spring, Chevy released the L78 396. This was essentially an updated Z-16, but with solid lifters and new exhaust manifolds. It had the 427-cid V-8's large-valve heads, plus 11.0:1 compression, aluminum intake manifold, and an 800-cfm Holley. The L78 echoed the Z-16's 375-bhp rating and was the 396 that hard-core Chevy street warriors had hoped all the '66s would be. Only about 3100 L78s were built. But even the base Chevelle SS was now a genuine big-block muscle car, and the best was yet to come.

Chevelle was restyled for '66, and all Super Sports now had a 396-cid V-8 of 325 or 360 bhp, or, like this one, the flashy 375-bhp L78. Note its unpainted aluminum intake manifold. The suspension was subpar, but the rest of the car delivered style and thrills at a modest price. The optional bucket-seat cabin features a console with clock and includes the extra-cost "knee-knocker" underdash tachometer. Redline tires were standard, but these pseudo-mag wheelcovers were optional in place of tiny "dog-dish" hub-caps.

Specifications

1966 Chevrolet Chevelle SS 396

Wheelbase, in. 115.0

Weight, lbs. 3700

Production 3100

Price $4300

Engine ohv V-8

Displacement, cid 396

Fuel system 1 × 4bbl.

Compression ratio 11.0:1

Horsepower @ rpm 375 @ 5600

Torque @ rpm 415 @ 3600

Representative performance

0-60 mph, sec. 6.0

¼ mile, sec. @ mph 14.40 @ 100

1966 Dodge
Charger 426 Hemi

*P*lymouth's 1964 Barracuda was America's first modern fast-back, beating Ford's '65 Mustang 2+2 to market by about two weeks. Dodge waited until '66 to join the fray, and then leaped in with muscle other fastbacks could only dream of.

Built on the mid-size Coronet platform, the new Charger added a rather graceless fastback roofline, hidden headlamps, and full-width taillamps. With a base price of $3122, it cost $417 more than a Coronet 500 hardtop. Part of the deal was a state-of-the-art '60s interior: lots of chrome, four bucket seats (the rears folded down), available center consoles fore and aft, and full gauges.

A 318-cid V-8 was standard. The most-common performance up-grade was the optional 325-bhp 383 four-barrel, which would push a Charger through the quarter in the low 16s at 85 mph. But 1966 was also the year Chrysler's 426-cid Hemi V-8 came to the streets, and it made for the ultimate Charger.

Actual horsepower was near 500, but Dodge advertised its Street Hemi at 425 bhp on a 10.25:1 compression. A detuned version of the 12.5:1-compression race Hemi, the new customer version retained solid lifters, but had a milder cam for smoother low-rpm running and a heat chamber so it could warm up properly. It also mounted its dual quads inline, rather than on a cross-ram manifold. The engine added $1000 to the price of a Coronet, or $880 to a Charger, and included stiffer springs and bigger (11-inch) brakes. Front discs were optional.

"Beauty and the beast," was how Dodge pitched its new Charger with the hot 426. "The Hemi was never in better shape," it boasted. Of 37,344 Chargers built for '66, however, only 468 got the Hemi. Maybe that's be-cause Hemi buyers got a one-year/12,000 warranty instead of Dodge's usual 5/50,000. Even that, Chrysler warned, would be voided if the car was "subjected to any extreme operation (i.e., drag racing)." Heaven forbid.

Dodge refitted a Coronet with a fastback roof, hidden-headlamp grille, and jet-age interior to create the Charger. Its cabin featured full instrumentation with a 150-mph speedometer and 6000-rpm tach, full-length console, and rear seatbacks that folded to create a cargo bay seven feet long. The new Street Hemi engine was a special-order option installed in just 468 '66 Chargers.

Specifications

1966 Dodge Charger 426 Hemi

Wheelbase, in. 117.0

Weight, lbs. 4500

Production 468

Price $5200

Engine ohv V-8

Displacement, cid 426

Fuel system 2 × 4bbl.

Compression ratio 10.25:1

Horsepower @ rpm 425 @ 5000

Torque @ rpm 490 @ 4000

Representative performance

0-60 mph, sec. 6.4

¼ mile, sec. @ mph 14.16 @ 96.15

1966 Ford Fairlane 427

"SCOOP!" screamed *Hot Rod*'s July 1966 cover. "Ford's new Street Fairlane with the BIG 427. First Report on the Wildest Car Ford Ever Built for You!" As it turned out, the glowing article that followed was about the most anyone ever saw of the '66 Fairlane 427.

Fords were being embarrassed at stoplights nationwide by the hottest GM and Chrysler intermediates. With its '66 redesign, the Fairlane finally had an engine bay large enough for big-cube power. GT versions got a 335-bhp 390-cid four-barrel and could turn mid-15s at around 90 mph in the quarter.

But respect on the street required more, so Ford turned to a detuned version of its racing 427-cid V-8. Running a medium-riser manifold, milder cam, and a few other street-friendly adjustments, it made 410 bhp with a four-barrel and 425 with dual quads.

Fitting the big, heavy 427 required relocated shock towers and larger front coil springs. Free-breathing cast-iron exhaust headers, low-re-

striction dual exhausts, and Ford's top-loader four-speed manual completed the powertrain.

Only two-door Fairlane 500s or 500XLs got the 427. Ordering it brought a lift-off fiberglass hood with functional air scoop. The only other exterior clue was a small fender insignia, though a Special Handling Package, manual front disc brakes, longer rear leaf springs, and larger bias-belted blackwall tires were part of the package. The interior was stock except for a 9000-rpm tach.

On the street, a 427 Fairlane was competitive with most anything the other guys had. Trouble was, the other guys had more of everything. The "wildest" Fairlane was expensive to build and couldn't be priced to sell in volume. Ford set its sights on Super Stock drag racing, where it need produce only 50 examples to qualify. It built no more than 70, and most went to pro racers. Ford street warriors were shortchanged again. At least *Hot Rod* did its part.

Specifications

1966 Ford Fairlane 427

Wheelbase, in. 116.0

Weight, lbs. 4100

Production 70

Price $5100

Engine ohv V-8

Displacement, cid 427

Fuel system 2 × 4bbl.

Compression ratio 11.1:1

Horsepower @ rpm 425 @ 6000

Torque @ rpm 480 @ 3700

Representative performance

0-60 mph, sec. 6.0

¼ mile, sec. @ mph 14.5 @ 100

Ford's best shot at a dominating street racer might have been the '66 Fairlane with a 427-cid V-8. Equipped like this one, with two 652-cfm Holley quads, the detuned race engine made 425 bhp. Its oval air cleaner breathed through the scooped lift-off fiberglass hood, which was secured by chrome pins. A mandatory four-speed manual augmented the stock Fairlane interior. Only 70 Fairlanes were built with the special-order 427 for '66. The engine became a regular-production option for '67, but fewer than 200 were installed.

1966 Oldsmobile
Cutlass 4-4-2

*T*hough its name identified the 4-4-2 as a collection of separate performance parts, no 1966 muscle intermediate had a more unified performance personality. Oldsmobile's interpretation of the modern supercar was quickly gaining a reputation as the best-balanced of the bunch.

New sheetmetal and a wider track marked changes to the Cutlass series for '66. The 4-4-2 still was an option on coupes and convertibles, adding just $185 to the price of an F-85 or $151 to a Cutlass. 4-4-2s got a unique grille, taillamps, and front-fender scoops. Bucket seats were standard on Cutlass versions, and sporty round gauges replaced the horizontal-sweep speedometer. A tach cost $52 extra.

Still exclusive to the 4-4-2 was the four-barrel 400-cid V-8. A slight hike in compression kicked horsepower to 350. For another $110, buyers could get Oldsmobile's first factory tri-carb setup since the late 1950s. It boosted output to 360 bhp and cut ETs to the high 14s at 97 mph. Olds had this one sorted out, and transition from the middle carb to the other two was smooth and manageable.

Shifting with the three- and four-speed manuals improved thanks to Hurst linkages, which were newly available from the factory and had both "4-4-2" and "Hurst" embossed on the gear lever.

A heavy-duty suspension with standard sway bars front and rear returned, and testers lauded the 4-4-2's road manners, saying it had a softer ride, yet better steering and control than the Chevelle SS and GTO. Braking was rated tops as well. Olds also began fitting in a few tri-power engines with the new W-30 system. It included an air-induction setup with scoops in the front bumper openings and also internal engine modifications.

For most 4-4-2s, the story was abundant power without orneriness, Olds comfort without sloppy handling, and nice equipment without exorbitant prices. "We would be hard put to find another car that does so many things so well," said *Motor Trend*.

1966 Oldsmobile Cutlass 4-4-2

Wheelbase, in. 115.0

Weight, lbs. 3600

Production 21,997

Price $3500

Engine ohv V-8

Displacement, cid 400

Fuel system 1 × 4bbl.

Compression ratio 10.5:1

Horsepower @ rpm 350 @ 3600

Torque @ rpm 440 @ 3600

Representative performance

0-60 mph, sec. 7.1

¼ mile, sec. @ mph 15.50 @ 91

A reskin that featured an elegant recessed back-light distinguished the '66 4-4-2, which was still an F-85/Cutlass option package. It included its own grille, taillamps, and fake front fender vents. A trifling compression hike brought five extra horses to the base 400-cid four-barrel (shown), though new tri-carb and W-30 air-induction options gave it 360 bhp or more. The 4-4-2 was well-bred compared to most super-cars. Even the Tri-Power variant "lacks, or perhaps one should say masks, the brutal nature which is apparent in some of the others," said Car Life.

1966 Plymouth
Satellite 426 Hemi

*C*hrysler offered its 426 Hemi engine briefly and in very limited numbers in some '65 Mopar intermediates, but with 12.5:1 compression and competition-grade tuning, it was too high-strung for the street. That changed in '66, when the 426-cid Hemi V-8 was added to the regular production options list.

Creating the Street Hemi required numerous changes to the race engine, including substituting cast-iron cylinder heads for aluminum ones and dual Carter four-barrels for the racing Holley carb. Among other alterations, the compression ratio was reduced to 10.25:1, a milder camshaft was installed, and a choke was added to the rear primaries so the engine could start in cold weather. As delivered from the factory, the race Hemi developed an estimated 550 bhp. The Street Hemi was rated at 425 bhp, though actual output was higher.

At Plymouth, the new engine found a home in the restyled Satellite and its less-plush Belvedere sibling. The Hemi was specially assembled at Chrysler's Marine/Industrial Division plant and ordering it added about $1000 to a Satellite two-door hardtop or convertible, pushing the price close to $4000 even without other options. Transmission choices were a four-speed manual or the TorqueFlite. The standard axle ratio with both was 3.23:1 and a Sure-Grip limited-slip diff was optional.

The engine came with a host of performance-enhancing extras, including heavy-duty suspension and police-grade 11-inch drum brakes (the front discs available in full-size Mopars weren't offered). Still, the nose-heavy Hemi Satellite was sloppy in turns and took a long time to stop. Around-town fuel economy was 10-13 mpg.

None of that was unusual for a truly hot machine of the day, but finally, here was an ultra-supercar that wasn't also burdened with poor driveability. *Car and Driver* called the 1966 Hemi Satellite "the best combination of brute performance and tractable street manners we've ever driven...."

Specifications

1966 Plymouth Satellite 426 Hemi

Wheelbase, in. 116.0

Weight, lbs. 3800

Production 817

Price $3900

Engine ohv V-8

Displacement, cid 426

Fuel system 2 × 4bbl.

Compression ratio 10.25:1

Horsepower @ rpm 425 @ 5000

Torque @ rpm 490 @ 4000

Representative performance

0-60 mph, sec. 5.3

¼ mile, sec. @ mph 13.8 @ 104

Midsize Plymouths got pleasantly reserved new styling for '66, but looks were the only thing understated about a Satellite equipped with the new 426 Street Hemi. "They supply the car, you supply the courage," said Car and Driver. *The Hemi went into 1521 '66 Plymouths, mostly Satellite hardtops. Buckets and console were standard, but the optional tach was mounted too low for easy reading.*

1966 Pontiac GTO

*R*ecognizing the GTO's growing popularity, Pontiac promoted it from a Tempest option to a model of its own for '66. The Goat rewarded Pontiac with sales of 96,946 units, the highest one-year total ever attained by a true muscle car.

Credit for its success was twofold. Other GM divisions had copied the GTO with hotter versions of their intermediates, but like Ford's new Fairlane GT, none captured the Goat's all-around appeal. Mopar had the performance, but no special muscle models. And while all GM mid-size cars were restyled for '66, none matched the beauty of the GTO's voluptuous new Coke-bottle contours.

Wheelbase was untouched, and overall length and curb weights changed negligibly. But styling highlights included a graceful new roofline and cool fluted taillamps. The unique GTO grille had mesh-pattern inserts made of plastic—an industry first.

The standard hood scoop remained nonfunctional, but Tri-Power en-

gines could again get an over-the-counter fresh-air kit, and a few were equipped with the Goat's first factory Ram Air. A small number of GTOs were ordered with a boss new option: weight-reducing red plastic inner fender liners. Inside, the new instrument-surround was genuine wood.

The four-barrel 389 continued at 335 bhp. The $113 triple-two-barrel had 360 bhp (with or without Ram Air), but production ceased at midyear when GM outlawed multi-carb engines for all but the Corvette. Three- and four-speed manuals and a two-speed automatic could be had with factory axles spanning 3.08:1 to 4.33:1.

Car Life's four-speed four-barrel with 3.08 gears and air conditioning ran a 15.4 quarter at 92 mph and got 12.4 mpg. The magazine said the lightly loaded rear wheels of its nose-heavy test car would "skitter and skip on anything but the driest pavement." Braking power was poor, but the shifter was sweet, the motor willing, and assembly quality high. That, and that beautiful new body, obviously was the formula for success in '66.

Specifications

1966 Pontiac GTO

Wheelbase, in. 115.0

Weight, lbs. 3950

Production 19,045

Price $3600

Engine ohv V-8

Displacement, cid 389

Fuel system 3 × 2bbl.

Compression ratio 10.75:1

Horsepower @ rpm 360 @ 5200

Torque @ rpm 424 @ 3600

Representative performance

0-60 mph, sec. 6.5

¼ mile, sec. @ mph 14.65 @ 98

Pontiac's was the shapeliest restyled '66 GM intermediate, and the GTO became its own model. Fluted lamps dressed up its tail, and a few cars got red plastic front fender liners. This is one of 19,045 ordered with Tri-Power before GM killed the option at midyear. Buckets and real wood dash trim were standard; the console was optional with any floor shifter.

1966 Pontiac 2+2

*I*t was clear to most enthusiasts by 1966 that midsize cars had seized the muscle mantle. Detroit, however, was reluctant to relinquish its time-tested biggest-car/best-engine formula. Given that, it was no accident that the leader in intermediate muscle also put together the finest full-size performance machine.

Pontiac first offered the 2+2 as a Catalina engine, suspension, and trim group in 1964. For '65, the 421-cid V-8 became a standard part of the option package, and for '66, Pontiac made the 2+2 a separate model, still based on the Catalina two-door hardtop or convertible. Flamboyantly styled and expansively proportioned, the 2+2 was unbeatable for sheer presence. It also could hold its own against a range of performance cars.

The basic package included the heavy-duty suspension, with even stiffer springs and shocks available. Buckets and a console were added to the top-line Catalina interior, which could be optioned with a sport steering wheel and instrumentation that included a tachometer and oil-pressure gauge. Unique exterior features included "2+2" badges, twin-

lens taillamps, and chrome bodyside gills; Pontiac's famous eight-lug aluminum wheels were the ultimate optional touch.

This was the only Poncho with standard 421-cid power. The 338-bhp four-barrel was the base engine. Two tri-power 421s were optional, one with 356 bhp, the other with 376. The last was the 421 HO and included a high-output camshaft and valve train. It used a declutching fan, special exhaust manifolds, and chrome low-restriction air cleaners; rocker covers and oil-filler cap also were chrome. Transistorized ignition was available. A three-speed stick was standard; a four-speed and automatic cost extra. The manuals had Hurst shifters. A limited-slip differential and gearing up to 4:11.1 were optional.

Calling into play enormous power and a decent 55/45 weight distribution, the 2+2 could be launched with little tire spin and guided through corners with alarming efficiency. And it cruised silently and rode with less harshness than muscle intermediates. The 2+2 reverted to option status for '67, then died, a proud relic of a time when big cars, Pontiacs in particular, ruled the streets.

Specifications

1966 Pontiac 2+2

Wheelbase, in. 121.0

Weight, lbs. 4550

Production 6383

Price $4600

Engine ohv V-8

Displacement, cid 421

Fuel system 3 × 2bbl.

Compression ratio 10.75:1

Horsepower @ rpm 376 @ 5000

Torque @ rpm 461 @ 3600

Representative performance

0-60 mph, sec. 7.0

¼ mile, sec. @ mph 15.4 @ 93

A 2+2 was Big Fun. It was the only Pontiac with standard 421-cid power; this one has the 376-bhp Tri-Power option and automatic transmission; the tach is an aftermarket item. No breakout exists on how many of the 6383 2+2s built for '66 were convertibles.

1967 Buick
GS 400

*B*uick's muscle machine stopped living its little lie for 1967, and was the better car for it.

Gone was the 401-cid V-8 that had masqueraded as a 400-cid mill. The car got a genuine 400-cid V-8 (well, actually 399.748 cid), and marked the occasion by a change in name, from Gran Sport to the GS 400.

Its hood scoops now faced forward, but still were decorative. The dashboard remained unsporting, and though a tachometer was a $47 option, it was mounted too low to read easily. With prices the highest of GM's four muscle intermediates, sales were slow. But for those willing to think in terms of all-around performance, the GS 400 delivered.

Like the top version of the 401, the 400 had 10.25:1 compression, hydraulic lifters, and 340 bhp. But the new engine was of a more-modern design, smoother running, higher-revving, and easier to keep in tune. It even had a futuristic plastic air cleaner.

Helping get the most from the new V-8 was a new optional automatic transmission with three speeds instead of two. Most testers preferred it to the three- or four-speed manuals, despite its extra $237 cost and 58 pounds of weight. Manually upshifting the automatic's console-mounted gear lever to second at 5600 rpm and to third at 4800, *Car Life* claimed a 0-60 mph time of 6.0 seconds and a 14.7-second quarter-mile at 97 mph with its 3.90:1 Positraction hardtop.

GS 400s came as two-door hardtops, pillared coupes, and convertibles, all with the ragtop's stouter frame. Chassis solidity was notable, and with newly standard F70x14 wide-oval tires, handling was among the best in class. Stopping ability was, too, thanks to power front disc brakes, a new $147 option.

Sales languished, however. Sympathized *Car Life*: "Buick's GS 400 series must be the best-kept secret in the youth/performance market—though undoubtedly it wasn't planned that way. . . ."

Specifications

1967 Buick GS 400

Wheelbase, in. 115.0

Weight, lbs. 3857

Production 2140

Price $3997

Engine ohv V-8

Displacement, cid 400

Fuel system 1 × 4bbl.

Compression ratio 10.25:1

Horsepower @ rpm 340 @ 5000

Torque @ rpm 440 @ 3200

Representative performance

0-60 mph, sec. 6.5

¼ mile, sec. @ mph 15.20 @ 95

Buick dropped the 401-cid V-8 and renamed its Gran Sport the GS 400 in honor of its new 400-cid mill, which wore a red plastic air cleaner. Of nearly 14,000 GS 400s built for '67, just 2140 were convertibles. Options on this one include bucket seats, four-speed manual, and a console-mounted tachometer. Buick said the new steering wheel's thick "tongue" spoke provided impact cushioning in a crash. Hood scoops now faced forward, but still weren't functional.

1967 Chevrolet Camaro SS 396

GM spotted Ford more than two years and 1.3 million Mustangs before answering the pony-car challenge. When it did, the Chevrolet Camaro and Pontiac Firebird had instant muscle credibility.

From the start, Camaro featured a Super Sport edition as an authoritative counterpunch to the Mustang GT. It added $211 to the $2572 Camaro Sport Coupe or the $2809 convertible. Included were firmer springs and shocks, wide-oval tires, a special hood with die-cast simulated louvers, and a bumblebee stripe around the car's nose. Many buyers combined it with the $105 Rally Sport package, which included hidden headlamps.

A new 295-bhp four-barrel 350-cid V-8 was the standard SS engine. With a four-speed and 3.31:1 gears, *Motor Trend*'s SS 350 ran 0-60 in 8 seconds and the quarter in 15.4 at 90 mph. That was directly comparable to a 335-bhp 390-cid Mustang GT.

Then, a few months into the model year, Chevy unleashed the SS 396.

It initially came in 325-bhp tune and tacked $263 onto the SS group. Still later in the year, the 375-bhp L78 variant was offered for $500. Since the L78 violated GM's rule against any car except the Corvette exceeding 10-bhp-per horsepower, it technically was listed as a dealer-installed option. (A few high-performance dealers also would install a 400-bhp-plus 427-cid V-8.) SS 396 Camaros came standard with a four-speed manual; the three-speed automatic was a $226 option.

With inadequate single-leaf rear springs and a near-vertical mounting of the rear shock absorbers, all V-8 Camaros were handicapped by severe rear-wheel hop in hard acceleration. With more weight over the nose and additional torque, the 396s suffered even more. But no rival was quicker.

First-year Camaro sales trailed Mustang by a wide margin, but of the 220,917 sold, more than 34,000 were Super Sports. Chevy's pony car was off and running.

Specifications

1967 Chevrolet Camaro SS 396

Wheelbase, in. 108.1

Weight, lbs. 3720

Production NA

Price $3700

Engine ohv V-8

Displacement, cid 396

Fuel system 1 × 4bbl.

Compression ratio 10.25:1

Horsepower @ rpm 325 @ 4800

Torque @ rpm 410 @ 3200

Representative performance

0-60 mph, sec. 6.0

¼ mile, sec. @ mph 14.5 @ 99

Camaro came in Super Sport form right from its '67 debut. Strongest of the bunch was the SS 396, this one a 325-bhp version. Stiffened suspension, F70x14 tires, dummy hood vents, woodgrain steering wheel and bumblebee nose stripe were part of the SS package. Here, it's combined with the Rally Sport option, which included inward-sliding vacuum-operated flaps over the headlamps. Rear spoiler, automatic trans, and console gauges are among the options.

1967 Chevrolet
Camaro Z-28

*T*he Sports Car Club of America's Trans American sedan series was the premier racing showcase for pony cars in the late '60s, and Chevy had to score there to hurt the entrenched Mustang.

Trans Am racers were production-based cars with engines of 305 cid or less. Chevy worked a forged steel version of the 283-cid V-8's crankshaft into its 327 V-8 to get 302 cid. Big-port Corvette heads, solid lifters, a hot cam, a baffled oil pan, and a Holley four-barrel on a tuned aluminum manifold were specified. Horsepower was rated at 290; it likely was close to 400.

At least 1000 streetable examples had to be produced, and Chevy's tack was to make the 302 part of a Camaro Regular Production Option Code. So low-key was the effort that the car wasn't advertised, or even mentioned in sales literature. The knowledgeable buyer had to order a base 6-cylinder Camaro ($2466), then scan the order sheet for what turned out to be the most famous RPO in history: Z28.

The package cost $400 and included the 302, the F-41 handling suspension, 15-inch tires on Corvette six-inch Rally wheels, and quick-ratio manual steering. A Muncie four-speed was the only transmission; power front disc brakes were a mandatory $100 option.

RPO Z28 was available on the coupe only and could be combined with the hidden-headlamp RS option group. There were no Z28 emblems on the car, but the package did include broad racing stripes on the hood and trunklid. Camaro's rear lip spoiler was a popular option.

The Z28 had a buckboard ride and sports-car handling. The 302 was a peaky devil, hard to launch and lethargic under 4000 rpm. Driven as it was meant to be, performance was shattering. *Road & Track* settled on 7500 rpm (!) as the optimal shift point and reported 63 mph in first gear, 85 in second, and 113 in third. Top speed approached 140 mph. "If the Z-28 isn't a bona fide racing car," said the magazine, "then we've never seen one."

Specifications

1967 Chevrolet Camaro Z28

Wheelbase, in. 108.1

Weight, lbs. 3500

Production 602

Price $3500

Engine ohv V-8

Displacement, cid 302

Fuel system 1 × 4bbl.

Compression ratio 11.0:1

Horsepower @ rpm 290 @ 5800

Torque @ rpm 290 @ 4200

Representative performance

0-60 mph, sec. 6.9

¼ mile, sec. @ mph 14.85 @ 101

Chevy's counterpunch to the Mustang in Trans Am warfare was the Z28, and it had to build a version for the street. Presented as an option for Camaro coupes, the original Z28 was without exterior identification except for fat racing stripes. It had a solid-lifter 302-cid V-8, four-speed manual, and a competition-grade suspension.

1967 Chevrolet Chevelle SS 396

The Chevelle SS 396 took several steps forward and a couple steps back for '67.

Advancements came mainly in road manners and driveability. Replacing the standard rayon two-ply 7.75x14 tires were lower-profile F70x14s with nylon belts. Grip and steering response improved, and the car felt more secure in changes of direction. The Wide Ovals also helped get the most out of the newly available front disc brakes, a $79 option that enhanced stopping power and pedal modulation. Accompanying the discs were purposeful-looking new 14-inch slotted wheels.

A three-speed manual was again the standard transmission, with a four-speed costing $105 more. The two-speed Powerglide automatic returned as a $116 extra, but for the first time, the three-speed Turbo Hydra-matic was offered. It cost $231 and was a quantum leap over the Powerglide, particularly in its ability to kick down promptly for better passing response.

Federal safety regulations brought an energy-absorbing steering column and padded instrument-panel surfaces, but the dashboard still was boring compared to, say, the GTO's. At least the optional tach was relocated from just above the driver's right knee to left of the steering wheel. Exterior changes were minor, with a slightly reworked bumper and grille and a blackout tail panel. The hood louvers remained nonfunctional.

A 325-bhp version of the 396-cid V-8 was again standard, but the $105 L34 upgrade lost 10 bhp, to 350, because of GM's new edict against any car but Corvette having more than one bhp per 10 pounds of curb weight. In a second underhood reversal, the 375-bhp L78 was no longer listed in sales brochures, but did remain a $476 dealer-installed conversion fitted into 612 cars.

All in all, Chevy had improved the SS 396. And with prices starting at $2825 for the coupe and $3033 for the ragtop—just about $285 more than comparable Malibu models—it was affordable, too.

Better tires, available front disc brakes, and a three-speed automatic improved the '67 SS 396. This is one of about 17,000 ordered with the 350-bhp 396, though Chevy's records don't show how many of the 63,006 SS 396 Chevelles built for '67 were ragtops. Options on this one include the $111 buckets seats, $32 sport steering wheel, and $47 tachometer, which was moved from under the dash to left of the speedometer. The power-bulge hood vents looked good, but weren't functional.

Specifications

1967 Chevrolet Chevelle SS 396

Wheelbase, in. 115.0

Weight, lbs. 3800

Production 17,176

Price $3200

Engine ohv V-8

Displacement, cid 396

Fuel system 1 × 4bbl.

Compression ratio 10.25:1

Horsepower @ rpm 350 @ 5200

Torque @ rpm 415 @ 3400

Representative performance

0-60 mph, sec. 6.5

¼ mile, sec. @ mph 15.3 @ 94

1967 Chevrolet
Chevy II Nova SS

*P*erhaps the toughest little overachiever ever to harass the traditional muscle intermediates was Chevy's Nova Super Sport. Never a style leader, this was the compact for the serious enthusiast who wanted to go fast on guile and light weight.

The Chevy II bowed for 1962, with Nova its deluxe edition. SS standing came the following year as part of a trim package, and by '65, a 300-bhp 327-cid V-8 was available. A redesign for '66 replaced the nerdy box shape with huskier contours. Super Sports were back as two-door hardtops with bucket seats and a pair of 327s: One had 275 bhp; the other was Chevy's killer 350-bhp variant, the L79.

When the Nova SS returned for '67, a base price of just $2683 landed the 275-bhp 327, but the L79 was not listed as an official factory offering. A handful did make it into the '67s, however, bringing the two-year run to about 2200 L79 Chevy IIs. Besides Super Sports, the engine also went into Novas and base Chevy IIs.

These were the guerrilla fighters of the muscle jungle. A low profile and a high power-to-weight ratio were their secret. The Super Sport edition had some extra chrome, blackout trim details, and small SS emblems. But even with the slotted wheels of the '67 disc-brake option, a Nova SS by no means shouted "hot car." Hooked to the mandatory four-speed manual transmission and carrying just 10 pounds per bhp, the tough L79 would quickly wind to near 6000 rpm, catching the big-cube glamour boys napping.

"The 350-bhp 327 in approximately Corvette tune, dropped into a Chevy II, didn't have the jukebox magic of a 409 or a 427," reminisced *Car and Driver*'s Patrick Bedard in his 1990 ranking of the best all-time street racers. "Still, that combination made for one the sneakiest muscle cars ever built . . . You might not notice a Chevy II in traffic until he got half a car-length on you. Even in a boss machine, you might have to run 80 or 90 mph to get it back. That's how fast those Chevy IIs were."

Specifications

1967 Chevrolet Chevy II Nova SS

Wheelbase, in. 110.0

Weight, lbs. 3000

Production 300

Price $3000

Engine ohv V-8

Displacement, cid 327

Fuel system 1 × 4bbl.

Compression ratio 11.0:1

Horsepower @ rpm 350 @ 5800

Torque @ rpm 360 @ 3600

Representative performance

0-60 mph, sec. 6.5

¼ mile, sec. @ mph 14.9 @ 96.5

The modest little Chevy II was a giant-killer when equipped with the 350-bhp 327-cid V-8. It was offered in all Chevy II series models, including this top-line Super Sport hardtop. SS Novas had specific exterior trim, including a black-accented grille. The slotted wheels came with front disc brakes, a new option for '67. Strato buckets were standard SS seats. The four-speed was a mandatory $184 option with the engine; the tachometer is aftermarket.

1967 Dodge Coronet R/T Hemi

*S*ometimes, packaging makes all the difference. Dodge's mid-size Coronet was given handsome new styling for '66 and could be armed with devastating power. But to casual eyes, the modest "426 Hemi" fender badge was all that separated it from grandpa's grocery-getter.

Dodge remedied that for '67, introducing a new model whose initials stood for Road and Track. Without disturbing the Coronet's clean lines, the R/T added enough performance cues to make its meaning clear. It got an exclusive Charger-inspired grille with exposed headlamps, plus modest nonfunctional hood slats and small R/T emblems. The sporty theme continued inside with standard bucket seats (though a tach was a $50 extra). Underneath, the R/T was all business: The suspension had heavy-duty everything—even ball joints—while the standard 11-inch police-spec drum brakes could be augmented by a $70 front-disc option.

Included in the $3199 base price of the R/T hardtop or the $3438 convertible was Chrysler's largest engine, the 440-cid V-8, here tweaked to 375 bhp and christened the Magnum. The only engine option was the 426-cid Hemi, now in its second year in "Street" trim and again rated at 425 bhp. It added $908. Transmission choices were Mopar's excellent heavy-duty three-speed TorqueFlite automatic or a four-speed manual.

For minimum-hassle street work, the consensus choice was the 440. It was quicker than the Hemi up to about 60 mph, cheaper to buy, and easier to maintain. But for pitiless dominance, it was the Hemi.

"The 426 Hemi is unquestionably the king of the muscle cars, both for its speed and for its defiance," wrote Patrick Bedard for *Car and Driver* in 1990, putting this edition of Mopar's intermediates among his Ten Best all-time muscle cars. "The 'Street Hemi' was a class act, very smooth, quiet at idle, tractable in traffic." Open it up, however, and it revved like a Ferrari and ruled like, well, King Kong.

Dodge conjured up the Coronet R/T—for Road and Track—as its first comprehensive muscle model. Standard was the new four-barrel 440 Magnum V-8. Dodge built 9553 '67 R/T hardtops and 628 convertibles; this is among 283 with the sole engine option, the 426 Hemi. Buckets were standard, and buyers chose between a center console with floor shift or a fold down center armrest with a column-shifted TorqueFlite, as shown here.

Specifications

1967 Dodge Coronet R/T Hemi

Wheelbase, in. 117.0

Weight, lbs. 4020

Production 283

Price $4000

Engine ohv V-8

Displacement, cid 426

Fuel system 2 × 4bbl.

Compression ratio 10.25:1

Horsepower @ rpm 425 @ 5000

Torque @ rpm 490 @ 4000

Representative performance

0-60 mph, sec. 4.8

¼ mile, sec. @ mph 13.5 @ 105

1967 Shelby GT 500

*T*o make a road-racing champ of Ford's 1965-66 Mustang, Carroll Shelby transformed it into a thundering thoroughbred ill-suited to everyday driving. By 1967, however, Shelby's audience was demanding more civility, and the original pony car was undergoing a revamp that finally gave it room for big-cube power.

Regular Mustangs could now get a 320-bhp 390-cid four-barrel V-8. Shelby, naturally, went further. His GT 350 retained its 289-cid V-8 with its 306-bhp rating, though deletion of tubular headers cut true output to about 290 bhp. And a new model, the GT 500, got a reworked 428-cid "Police Interceptor."

The 428 was otherwise reserved for bigger Fords, where it made 345 bhp. Shelby added a cast-aluminum 427 medium-riser intake manifold, twin 600-cfm Holley four-barrels, and other tweaks for a conservative rating of 355 bhp. During manufacture or through dealers, a handful of GT 500s got Ford's near-race 427-cid V-8s.

GT 500s had a four-speed manual or three-speed automatic, with axle ratios from 3.50:1 to 4.11:1. Instead of the competition-grade underpinnings, the suspension was a fortified version of the Mustang GT's, with standard front disc brakes and E70x15 tires. Also gone were the two-seat cabins and standard racing harnesses of the originals. All '67s had Mustang GT-level interior trim, and air conditioning and power steering were new factory options. An 8000-rpm tach, 140-mph speedometer, and padded roll bar, however, remained Shelby standards.

Fiberglass body pieces included an elongated nose, a hood with functional scoops, and four bodyside intakes. The fiberglass tail had a molded spoiler and sequential Cougar turn-signal lamps. High-beam lights were mounted in the center of the grille (some were moved to the sides to meet state laws). Twin "Le Mans" stripes were dealer-applied options.

If Shelby Mustangs were now less race car and more grand touring machine, that was fine with buyers, who took an immediate liking to the new GT 500. It cost just $200 more than the GT 350, and handily outsold its small-block companion by 875 units.

In just two years, Shelby's Mustangs had matured from un-tamed road racers to more-marketable adult sports cars, a change marked by arrival of the big-block GT 500 in '67. Aluminum air cleaner and valve covers embellished its dual-quad 428, while fiberglass modifications, including functional scoops and sequential turn-signal lamps, distinguished the body. Ten-spoke mags were Shelby exclusives. Three-spoke steering wheel, 140-mph speedometer, 8000-rpm tach, and shoulder harnesses were among the interior features.

Specifications

1967 Shelby GT 500

Wheelbase, in. 108.0

Weight, lbs. 3600

Production 2050

Price $5000

Engine ohv V-8

Displacement, cid 428

Fuel system 2 × 4bbl.

Compression ratio 10.5:1

Horsepower @ rpm 355 @ 5400

Torque @ rpm 420 @ 3200

Representative performance

0-60 mph, sec. 6.2

¼ mile, sec. @ mph 14.6 @ 99

1967 Mercury
Comet 427

*I*f Ford had trouble winning respect on the streets in the mid '60s, Mercury had it worse. It was ignored. All the better, then, when a 427 Comet showed up. Talk about a sleeper.

It took until '66 for the Comet to graduate from the Ford Falcon-based compact platform to the Fairlane's mid-size chassis. Cyclone versions were available with Ford's corporate 335-bhp 390-cid V-8, but being even heavier than the Fairlane GT, they were stones.

A few dozen '66 Fairlanes had been fitted with the no-excuses 427, but it wasn't until '67 that the engine became a regular-production option and was extended to the Comet line. Mercury made it available in any two-door Comet—the Cyclone, Caliente, and Capri hardtops, and the bottom-of-the-line Comet 202 pillared coupe. The last was an interesting subject. It was a half-foot shorter than the hardtops and 100 pounds lighter. It was dumpier looking, too, with its Falcon-like roofline.

Picture one with vanilla paint. Bench seats. Dog-dish hubcaps. No scoops. No stripes. Just a discreet "427" fender emblem. The perfect Q-ship.

As in the '67 Fairlane (where it was called the "Cobra 427"), the 427-cid V-8 was offered in two flavors. With a 780-cfm Holley four-barrel and 410 bhp, Mercury called it the "Cyclone 427." With dual 652-cfm Holley quads and 425 bhp, it was the "Super Cyclone 427." Both had 11.1:1 compression, solid lifters, and came only with a four-speed.

Just 200 or so '67 Fairlanes were ordered with the 427, and even fewer Comets. With the Super Cyclone powertrain, plus well-considered extras such as a tach ($47), wide-oval whitewall nylon tires ($83), and power front disc brakes ($84), a Comet 202 would have retailed for around $3200. Hottest big-block, lightest body, no frills—not even a radio. This was the muscle car distilled to its essence.

Specifications

1967 Mercury Comet 427

Wheelbase, in. 116.0

Weight, lbs. 3400

Production 5

Price $3200

Engine ohv V-8

Displacement, cid 427

Fuel system 2 × 4bbl.

Compression ratio 11.1:1

Horsepower @ rpm 425 @ 6000

Torque @ rpm 480 @ 3700

Representative performance

0-60 mph, sec. 6.0

¼ mile, sec. @ mph 14.3 @ 102

If the quintessential muscle car consists of the most-powerful big-inch V-8 in the lightest midsize body, then this Comet 202 defines the breed. The dual-quad 427-cid was a production option in Fairlanes and Comets for '67. Fewer than 300 were installed, and only five went into the entry-level 202 model, which was shorter and lighter than regular Comets. Only "427" badges on the fenders and a four-speed gearshift in the spartan cabin tipped its hand.

1967 Oldsmobile
Cutlass 4-4-2 W-30

*O*lds called its 1967 sporty cars the "Youngmobiles" and advertised them accordingly. Tires were "boots," styling was "with it," and the 4-4-2 was "the sweetest, neatest, completest anti-boredom bundle on rubber!" One ad touted the 4-4-2 as "Keeper of the Cool." That was quite accurate in the case of cars with the W-30 performance package.

Olds quietly shipped 54 of the setups in '66, but gave the W-30 Force-Air-Induction System more play for '67. Of 24,829 4-4-2s built that year, about 500 got the $300 option. The original W-30 application was for the 360-bhp tri-carb engine, but GM restricted multi-carb outfits to the Corvette in '67. All 4-4-2s now had the four-barrel 400-cid V-8, which retained its 350-bhp rating even in W-30 form—though power and torque peaked 400 rpm higher in W-30s.

The W-30 induction system was more efficient than scoops that simply captured air running over the hood. It drew cold air from unobtrusive inlets above and below the parking lights, then ran it through two four-inch hoses to a specially stamped air cleaner. Location of the inlets and arrangement of the ducting created a pressurizing effect.

To make room for the hoses, the battery was relocated to the trunk, which also helped weight distribution. W-30 engines weren't ignored, gaining a hotter cam, stronger valve springs, and higher oil pressure.

Newly optional front disc brakes enhanced road manners that already were tops in the muscle-car field. *Car and Driver* flat called it "the best-handling car of its type we've ever tested."

The optional two-speed automatic transmission was replaced by a more-responsive Hydra-matic three-speed tuned for high-rpm upshifts, cars with the optional 3.42:1 and 3.91:1 gears got a new, high-capacity rear axle, and durability of the optional Anti-Spin diff was improved.

As for the W-30 package, the name may have been merely an order code, but it soon became slang for the ultimate 4-4-2.

Specifications

1967 Oldsmobile Cutlass 4-4-2 W-30

Wheelbase, in. 115.0

Weight, lbs. 4200

Production 402

Price $4100

Engine ohv V-8

Displacement, cid 400

Fuel system 1 × 4bbl.

Compression ratio 10.5:1

Horsepower @ rpm 350 @ 5400

Torque @ rpm 440 @ 4000

Representative performance

0-60 mph, sec. 6.7

¼ mile, sec. @ mph 14.98 @ 95

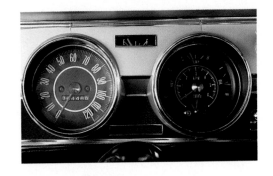

With Tri-Power outlawed by GM, all 4-4-2s used a four-barrel 400-cid V-8, and some got the dealer-installed W-30 system. Scoops in the headlight housing fed air to the carb through five-inch fabric tubes. All 4-4-2s had bucket seats; this one has the newly optional three-speed Hydra-matic automatic. Next to its speedometer is the optional—and confusing—tach/clock/amp/oil/coolant-temp gauge.

1967 Plymouth Belvedere GTX

*T*here were plenty of fast Plymouths before 1967, but none had the unified performance image pioneered by the Pontiac GTO. Plymouth addressed this for '67 with an executive-class hot rod that leaned a little on the Poncho for its name: GTX.

Based on the good-looking two-door Belvedere hardtop and convertible, the GTX dressed up with a special grille and tail panel, simulated hood scoops, and chrome gas cap. Twin racing stripes were optional. The cabin was top-of-the-line, with bucket seats, embossed vinyl, and lots of brightwork.

Going fast without fuss was the GTX's mission, so it got a standard powertrain capable of enormous power with minimal effort: Mopar's newly fortified 375-bhp 440-cid V-8. Plymouth called it the Super Commando 440. This was Chrysler's big-car engine improved for high-rpm performance with a revised camshaft and valve train, and free-flowing intake and exhaust systems.

Mopar's unassailable three-speed TorqueFlite automatic was standard. A four-speed manual was optional and came with some serious stuff, including a larger ring gear, double-breaker distributor, free-wheeling fan, even an oil-pan windage tray.

Six-leaf rear springs, plus heavy-duty shocks, torsion bars, and ball joints had critics praising the GTX's handling, though most found the optional power steering grossly overassisted. Disc brakes were optional, but surprisingly didn't seem to provide a great advantage over the standard heavy-duty drums.

Some 720 buyers forked over an additional $546 for the GTX's sole engine option, the 425-bhp 426 Street Hemi. It used the standard GTX running gear and could turn the quarter in the low-13s, but the 440/TorqueFlite was its equal in most street tussles. Plymouth finally had its image car, and it made no apologies to its inspiration. "GTO owners had better look to their defenses," counseled *Car and Driver*.

Plymouth finally took an encompassing approach to midsize muscle with the GTX. It came with buckets and a TorqueFlite that used a column or floor shifter. The new 375-bhp 440-cid four-barrel was standard. Options included a four-speed, center console, and the 426 Hemi. Plymouth built 11,429 GTX hardtops and 686 convertibles for '67; 720 of them with the Hemi. "Pit Stop" gas cap and fake hood vents were trendy touches.

1967 Pontiac Firebird 400

*P*ontiac led Detroit into the muscle age, but took a back seat when it came time for its first pony car. GM's pecking order gave Chevrolet first crack at the new F-body compact, and Camaro debuted for the '67 model year five months before the Firebird.

Saddled with the Camaro's wheelbase, chassis, and major body panels, Pontiac strove to give its car individuality. Firebird got the division's trademark split grille for 4.3-inches more overall length than the Camaro, plus GTO-inspired taillamps. An optional hood-mounted tachometer and mag-style Rally II wheels were unique to the Firebird. And interior appointments were a grade better, too. Pontiac even positioned each engine option as a separate model, designating base and Sprint 6-cylinder cars, the V-8 Firebird 326 and 326 HO, and the high-performance Firebird 400.

The last borrowed its 400-cid four-barrel from the GTO. Base and Ram Air versions were offered, each with chrome engine dress. Ram Air

cost $616 extra and breathed through the otherwise-decorative hood scoops. Both 400s were rated at 325 bhp and 410 lb-ft of torque, but the Ram Air's peak power came 400 rpm higher, at 5200 rpm.

A heavy-duty three-speed was standard, with a four-speed manual and three-speed Turbo Hydra-matic automatic optional. Performance axle ratios went with the four-speed: 3.55:1 was standard; up to 4.33:1 was available with Ram Air. A sport suspension and F70x14 tires were 400-model standards, with 11-inch front disc brakes a desirable option. Firebird had the same inadequate single-leaf rear springs as Camaro, but wheel-hop off the line was not nearly as severe thanks to mini-traction bars Pontiac fitted to all the 400 models.

Firebird prices ran about $200 over comparable Camaros, and the Chevy outsold it more than two-to-one for '67. But the Firebird 400 could hold its own against any pony car. So while Pontiac may have been outranked and outsold, it wasn't outdone.

Specifications

1967 Pontiac Firebird 400

Wheelbase, in. 108.1

Weight, lbs. 3800

Production 18,632

Price $3800

Engine ohv V-8

Displacement, cid 400

Fuel system 1 × 4bbl.

Compression ratio 10.75:1

Horsepower @ rpm 325 @ 4800

Torque @ rpm 410 @ 3400

Representative performance

0-60 mph, sec. 6.2

¼ mile, sec. @ mph 14.7 @ 98

Firebird alighted a few months after the comparable Camaro, positioned slightly upmarket of its Chevy cousin. Of 82,560 Pontiac built for '67, 18,632 were Firebird 400 models, which came as coupes or convertibles with a 400-cid V-8 borrowed from the GTO. Ram Air was an option that opened the otherwise decorative hood scoops. Three- and four-speed manuals were offered; this one has the optional automatic transmission.

1967 Pontiac GTO

*D*etails can mean so much. To their muscle car's pleasing nose, Pontiac designers added simple polished "chain link" grille inserts. At the tail, they resculpted some edges and cleaned up the lamps. Without disturbing the matchless lines of the '66, the stylists had created an aesthetic triumph—the 1967 GTO.

There was something fresh behind that gorgeous new grille: the standard engine was now a 400-cid enlargement of the 389-cid V-8. Compression was unchanged and the base four-barrel again made 335 bhp. But taking over the 360-bhp slot from the discontinued tri-carb setup was a new four-barrel High Output option. It cost $77 extra and added a higher-lift cam, free-flow exhaust manifolds, and an open-element air cleaner.

For another $263, the HO mill could be fitted with Ram Air. These ultimate GTO V-8s had extra-strong valve springs, a longer-duration cam, and were underrated at 360 bhp. The Ram Air package consisted of hardware that opened the otherwise nonfunctional hood scoops, plus a pan that went around the open-element air cleaner and mated to the hood with a foam-rubber skirt. Ram Air was a factory option ordered for 751 cars, but the pan and scoop parts were shipped in the trunk of the car for installation by the dealer. The owner was advised to refit the closed-scoop hardware during wet weather.

Hurst-shifted three- and four-speeds were the manual transmission offerings. Ram Air versions could use stick or automatic, but the 4.33:1 axle ratio was mandatory. Replacing the two-speed automatic was the three-speed Turbo Hydra-matic. When it was ordered with a center console, the gear lever was relocated from the steering column to the floor and a Hurst Dual Gate shifter was used. The driver could leave the lever in Drive, or slide it into an adjacent gate for fully manual shifting.

Among other new options were power front disc brakes ($105) and a hood-mounted tach ($84).

Specifications

1967 Pontiac GTO

Wheelbase, in. 115.0

Weight, lbs. 3900

Production 81,722

Price $3750

Engine ohv V-8

Displacement, cid 400

Fuel system 1 × 4bbl.

Compression ratio 10.75:1

Horsepower @ rpm 360 @ 51600

Torque @ rpm 438 @ 3600

Representative performance

0-60 mph, sec. 6.6

¼ mile, sec. @ mph 14.66 @ 99

Detail revisions fine-tuned the GTO's styling, while underhood, a 400-cid V-8 replaced the hallowed 389. Of 81,722 GTOs built for '67, this is one of 13,827 equipped with the 360-bhp High Output engine. It also has the optional hood-mounted tach, which looked cool, but was hard to read in rain or direct sunlight. The cabin was still top-flight, even if the dash did trade wood trim for a woodgrain vinyl appliqué.

1968 AMC AMX

*I*n 1968, a company previously unknown for high performance suddenly unveiled a model with enough appeal that it was embraced by two enthusiast groups: muscle car folks and sports-car people.

Inspired by the 1966 American Motors Experimental concept car, the AMX featured a big-cube V-8 for straight-line go, but had a wheelbase one-inch shorter than a Corvette's, and just two-seats—a combination that begged for twisty roads.

AMC created the AMX by slicing 12 inches of wheelbase from its new four-seat Javelin pony car. It gave the resulting 97-inch wheelbase coupe a bolder grille and a cleaner fastback roofline, plus a decorative power-dome hood. Carpeted panels replaced the rear bench, making the AMX and the 'Vette the only American-built two-seaters.

Upgrades from the standard 225-bhp 290-cid V-8 were a 280-bhp 343, and the most popular choice, a 315-bhp 390. The 390 shared the 343's heads, but had its own block, forged instead of cast crankshaft and con-

necting rods, and larger bearings. All AMX engines used a single four-barrel. A Borg-Warner four-speed was standard and a three-speed automatic with floor shift was optional. Factory axle ratios ranged from 2.87:1 to 3.54:1, with dealer-installed 4.10:1 and 5.00:1 gears available.

Underneath was a heavy-duty suspension, E70x14 tires, a beefy front sway bar, and a pair of trailing arms that acted like traction bars to fight rear-axle power hop. Twin racing stripes were optional, but each AMX got its production number set into the dashboard. AMC bragged that it would build no more than 8000 '68 AMXs, and this emphasized the limited-production nature of its two-seater.

An AMX couldn't stay with a Corvette in the curves, but was otherwise among the very best-handling domestic cars of its day. The four-speed's terrible shift linkage made the automatic the preferred transmission. But few other automobiles even attempted to blend American-style power with European-style handling, and do it at family-car prices.

Specifications

1968 AMC AMX

Wheelbase, in. 97.0

Weight, lbs. 3400

Production 4399

Price $3900

Engine ohv V-8

Displacement, cid 390

Fuel system 1 × 4bbl.

Compression ratio 10.2:1

Horsepower @ rpm 315 @ 4600

Torque @ rpm 425 @ 3200

Representative performance

0-60 mph, sec. 6.6

¼ mile, sec. @ mph 14.8 @ 95

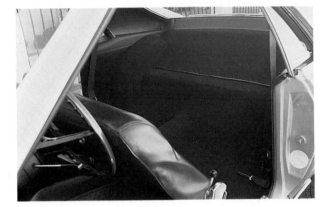

Hardly known for high performance, AMC scored with the AMX. It was basically a shortened Javelin with two seats, sporty instrumentation, a taut suspension, and standard V-8 power. Of 6725 built for '68, this is one of 4399 with the 315-bhp 390 four-barrel, the top engine choice.

1968 Buick GS 400

GM's mid-size lineup got new bodies and two-door models got a shorter, 112-inch wheelbase for 1968. That meant big styling changes for the muscle contingent, including the GS 400.

Buick gave its entry the long-hood, short-deck look that defined performance, but the aft flanks now looked quite massive. In fact, the new GS 400 weighed slightly more than the old, despite losing three inches of wheelbase and 4.4-inches of overall length.

That meant little change in acceleration, since powertrain choices were unaltered. And the trimmer size didn't seem to translate into stellar road manners; some testers said it plowed through turns worse than the '67 model. Finally, the dashboard retained an unsporting horizontal-sweep speedometer flanked by idiot lights.

But what do the critics know? The public liked the new GS 400, and sales held steady despite more and stronger rivals from within GM and without. To Buick's credit, it kept price increases modest, assembly quality high, and its upscale image intact.

"Priced and powered in line with its competition . . . the GS 400 is the most luxurious of the lot, yet takes a back seat to none in performance," maintained *Car Life* magazine.

Offered as a hardtop coupe and convertible, the GS 400 benefited from a standard 400-cid four-barrel that delivered strong seat-of-the-pants performance without the peakiness and fussiness of most high-output engines. Transmission alternatives to the standard three-speed were a four-speed manual or three-speed automatic. Positraction, front disc brakes, and power steering were options.

To those who wanted more, Buick offered a dealer-installed package that imbued the engine with a hotter cam, 11.0:1 compression, and stronger valve springs, and gave the transmission high-upshift modifications. Despite a 345-bhp rating it added an estimated 50 bhp and cut quarter-mile times by a second or more. The name of this rare dealer-installed option was a portent of great things to come from Buick. It was called the "Stage 1 Special Package."

Specifications

1968 Buick GS 400

Wheelbase, in. 112.0

Weight, lbs. 4030

Production 10,743

Price $4100

Engine ohv V-8

Displacement, cid 400

Fuel system 1 × 4bbl.

Compression ratio 10.25:1

Horsepower @ rpm 340 @ 5000

Torque @ rpm 440 @ 3200

Representative performance

0-60 mph, sec. 6.8

¼ mile, sec. @ mph 15.2 @ 92

Buick's midsize two-doors and their GS 400 performance iteration shed sedan proportions for the fashionable long-hood, short-deck look in '68. GS 400s came with these chrome-plated wheel covers and simulated fender air extractors. Bucket seats, center console, and automatic transmission with stirrup shifter were optional sporty touches, but Buick kept the dashboard design quite conservative. The standard 340-bhp 400-cid V-8 was strong on mid-range torque and performed without the peakiness typical of most hot engines. Buick built 10,743 GS 400 hardtops and 2454 GS 400 convertibles for '68.

1968 Chevrolet Camaro SS 396

*R*efinement was the byword for Camaro's second season. Astro-Ventilation, which circulated fresh air though the interior, spelled the demise of the vent wing windows. And new federal regulations brought on side-marker lights.

Super Sport equipment added just $210 to a coupe or convertible and again included a heavy-duty suspension and the 285-bhp 350-cid V-8. For another $52, buyers could get the 325-bhp version of the 396-cid V-8, while an additional $240 or so netted the 375-bhp L78. Splitting the difference in price and power was a new 350-bhp version of the 396. About 270 396s received special-order aluminum cylinder heads and earned the L89 badge, but saw no change to the 375-bhp rating.

Axle tramp was diminished with the addition of staggered rear shocks to all Camaros, while SS models got the additional benefits of five-leaf rear springs. The front disc brake option again included slotted Rally wheels in 14- and 15-inch sizes. Positraction remained a $42 extra. The SS 396 gained its own hood with dual banks of four nonfunctional ports, and was the only Camaro Super Sport with a blackout tail panel. The hidden-headlamp Rally Sport package returned at $105.

Inside, Camaros ordered with the Turbo Hydra-matic three-speed automatic got a stirrup-shaped shifter. And the optional rev-counter and clock could be combined into a gauge Chevy called the "Tick-Tock Tach."

Despite stronger competition, Camaro sales increased by 14,198 units for '68, to 235,147. That still trailed Mustang overall, but Camaro was the more-popular ride among performance enthusiasts and SS models accounted for about 12 percent of its sales.

For those who wanted more than even an SS 396 could deliver, a few high-performance Chevy dealers, such as Nicky in Chicago and Baldwin in New York, were already fitting a handful of '67 and '68 Camaros with 427-cid Corvette engines. These were $6000 Camaros, and they were devastating street machines.

Specifications

1968 Chevrolet Camaro SS 396

Wheelbase, in. 108.1

Weight, lbs. 3725

Production 10,773

Price $3800

Engine ohv V-8

Displacement, cid 396

Fuel system 1 × 4bbl.

Compression ratio 10.25:1

Horsepower @ rpm 325 @ 4800

Torque @ rpm 410 @ 3200

Representative performance

0-60 mph, sec. 6.6

¼ mile, sec. @ mph 15.0 @ 94

Camaros lost their wing windows and gained side-marker lights for '68. Super Sport equipment was available on coupes and convertibles. Of roughly 28,000 SS Camaros built this year, 18,199 were SS 396s. This 325-bhp edition was the most-popular 396, going into 10,773 cars. Decorative hood vents were a new SS 396 feature, as was the stirrup-like shifter for automatic models.

1968 Chevrolet
Chevelle SS 396

*T*he 1968-70 Chevelle Super Sport was as close to an Every-man's muscle car as Detroit would ever get. Reliable and affordable, it outsold every other true high-performance machine of the day, and beat its share, to boot.

Two-door GM intermediates lost three inches of wheelbase and gained shapely new styling for '68. Chevy's midsize muscle mainstay returned with 396-cid V-8 power, heavy-duty suspension, and F70x14 wide-ovals for a list price of just $2875. The interior was revamped, but bucket seats were a $111 option. Power front disc brakes ($100), Positraction ($42), and accent stripes ($30) were popular extras.

The base Turbo-Jet 396 again had 325 bhp, with $105 more buying the 350-bhp L34 version. Returning to the official options list for the first time since late 1966 was the lusty 375-bhp L78. It had solid lifters, big-port heads, and an 800-cfm Holley four-barrel on a low-rise aluminum manifold—all for a reasonable $237. A three-speed manual was

standard with all engines, and a four-speed or automatic were optional. Axle ratios began with 2.73:1 highway gearing and ended with dealer-installed 4.88:1 drag cogs.

Chevy still didn't seem to have the SS 396's suspension sorted out: It rode harshly yet allowed the nose to porpoise over bumps. And the Muncie four-speed didn't shift with near the smoothness of the Hurst linkages offered as original equipment on some competitors.

But with the L78 in its holster, an SS 396 was a match for most anything coming out of rival showrooms. It idled roughly but revved ferociously. Remembered Patrick Bedard in a 1990 *Car and Driver* retrospective of top muscle cars: "If you came up beside an SS 396 in those days, you listened carefully. If you heard sixteen little hammers, the racket of solid lifters, you knew the guy was dangerous."

Chevy built 62,785 SS 396 Chevelles for '68. A fraction were ordered with the L78, but that engine wasn't for every man.

Specifications

1968 Chevrolet Chevelle SS 396

Wheelbase, in. 112.0

Weight, lbs. 4160

Production 4751

Price $3700

Engine ohv V-8

Displacement, cid 396

Fuel system 1 × 4bbl.

Compression ratio 11.0:1

Horsepower @ rpm 375 @ 5600

Torque @ rpm 415 @ 3600

Representative performance

0-60 mph, sec. 6.5

¼ mile, sec. @ mph 14.5 @ 100

Chevy's SS 396 became America's most-popular muscle car thanks in large part to the new styling it got for '68. Most were hardtops (just 2286 convertibles were built), and some, like this 375-bhp L78, came dressed down and ready to rumble. But there were sore spots. The suspension was too soft, the in-dash tachometer was hard to read, and shifting suffered because the Muncie four-speed's linkage was attached to a frame member and became misaligned under power.

1968 Dodge
Charger R/T Hemi

*M*opar fans still bristle at the thought of Steve McQueen's 390 Mustang besting that black 440 Charger R/T. At least producers of the hit film *Bullitt* knew what they were doing when they cast the redesigned Dodge as McQueen's foil. The car had star quality.

Charger's new hidden-headlamp grille, curvy body, elegant recessed backlight, refined tail, and spare use of chrome represented a styling high point for '60s muscle cars. And in R/T form, its performance justified equal praise.

For $3506, the R/T came with the 375-bhp 440-cid four-barrel Magnum V-8, heavy-duty brakes, R/T handling package, and F70x14 tires. The rear bumblebee stripe could be left off, while inside, the original Charger's space-age interior gave way to less-flashy, functional decor.

The only engine option was the mighty 426 Hemi, at $605. Chrysler strengthened it for '68, with a slightly longer-duration cam, new valve springs, and revisions that reduced oil consumption. It was still underrated at 425 bhp, but as *Car and Driver* marvelled, "There just isn't

more honest horsepower available off the showroom floor than you get from this bright orange monster."

Either engine could be hooked to a TorqueFlite automatic with a floor lever or a four-speed with a Hurst Competition-Plus shifter. Automatic was the ticket for straight-line acceleration, and Hemi cars got a special high-stall-speed torque converter (3.23:1 gears were standard). The driver could upshift at 6500 rpm, or let the TorqueFlite do it at 5500. In traffic, the Hemi could be driven like a docile small-block, yet was more than half a second quicker and 10 mph faster in the quarter-mile than a 440 Charger.

The '68 model's new bucket seats lacked support, and its flying-buttress roof pillars reduced rear visibility. On R/Ts, handling was a nose-heavy chore, and such essential items as a tach, power front disc brakes, and power steering were options. Still, Charger sales increased sixfold over '67, leaving just one question: How would McQueen have done against a Hemi?

Specifications

1968 Dodge Charger R/T Hemi

Wheelbase, in. 117.0

Weight, lbs. 4300

Production 475

Price $4800

Engine ohv V-8

Displacement, cid 426

Fuel system 2 × 4bbl.

Compression ratio 10.25:1

Horsepower @ rpm 425 @ 5000

Torque @ rpm 490 @ 4000

Representative performance

0-60 mph, sec. 5.3

¼ mile, sec. @ mph 13.8 @ 105

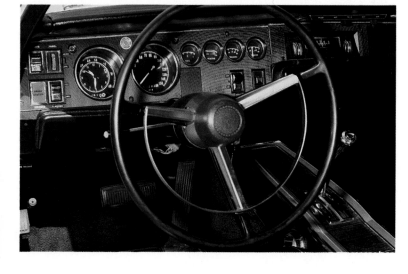

The second-generation Charger was one of the day's handsomest muscle cars, aptly described by Car and Driver *as "all guts and purpose." Of 92,590 produced for '68, 17,665 were R/T versions. The 440 Magnum V-8 was standard on R/Ts. This is one of 475 ordered with the optional 426 Hemi (and one of 264 Hemis with TorqueFlite). The prominent gas cap was a racing-inspired styling touch, while the instrument panel showed some enthusiast influence as well, though a tachometer was a $49 option. The bumblebee stripes could be left off if the buyer desired.*

1968 Dodge Dart GTS 440

*T*he ultimate street-racer's fantasy is to show up in a ratty-looking sleeper and blow off everyone's doors. A 440 Dart made that a reality for at least one bold fellow. You could look it up.

With its standard 340-cid V-8, the '68 Dart GTS was a worthy member of Dodge's new performance-car group, the Scat Pack. Underrated at 275 bhp, a GTS could turn mid-14s at 99 mph. The optional 383 V-8 had 335 bhp, but weight disadvantages meant it wasn't much quicker than the nimbler 340.

Of course, that didn't stop some Mopar freaks from stuffing in a 440-cid V-8. In all, about 650 '68 and '69 Darts were fitted with the big-block Magnum, which almost always was modified after the transplant to well beyond its 375-bhp factory rating. Conversion of a group of 48 '68 GTSs was typical.

Dodge shipped 383-spec Darts (minus powertrain) along with factory-prepped 440 engines to Hurst-Campbell, Inc. a Michigan after-market company. Hurst-Campbell did the conversion, Dodge reps inspected it, and the cars were forwarded to Grand Spaulding Auto Sales in Chicago, a performance-oriented Dodge dealer. These cars got vehicle identification numbers, but were not covered by the factory warranty.

With even more weight in front and no power steering (it wouldn't fit), 440 Darts were good for little but all-out straight-line attacks. So irresistible was the setup that a thief stole *Car and Driver*'s brand-new, bright-blue 440 Dart test car from its New York parking space.

Documenting the heist in its October 1969 issue, the magazine said the Dart soon surfaced "at a local street racing highway and cleaned up. The car, camouflaged in light gray primer…had put down a brace of Corvettes that had gained some local renown."

The thief was eventually caught red-handed at New York National Speedway, where the Dart was embarrassing all rivals. Appropriately enough, it was running in the dragway's "Hot Car" class.

Specifications

1968 Dodge Dart GTS 440

Wheelbase, in. 111.0

Weight, lbs. 3600

Production 48

Price $4000

Engine ohv V-8

Displacement, cid 440

Fuel system 1 × 4bbl.

Compression ratio 10.1:1

Horsepower @ rpm 375 @ 4600

Torque @ rpm 480 @ 3200

Representative performance

0-60 mph, sec. 5.0

¼ mile, sec. @ mph 13.3 @ 107

Showroom Dart GTSs got Mopar's fine 340- or 383-cid V-8s, but a few were special-fitted with the big 440 Magnum. These were street-legal cars, but aftermarket headers, ignition kit, hoses, wiring, air cleaner, and internal hop-ups on this 440 are typical of the drag-racing modifications most of them got. And wait, there's more. About 80 Darts were fitted with the 426 Hemi. Note that this car retains "383" badges.

1968 Dodge Super Bee

GM divisions had practiced it for years, but it took the competitive fervor of the muscle years to spark a sibling rivalry between Dodge and Plymouth. Plymouth struck first with the fall '67 introduction of the budget-muscle 1968 Road Runner. Dodge—already irked that it had coined the "road runner" name in a '67 Coronet R/T advertisement—scrambled to respond.

Its answer was a bang-for-the-buck stripper based on the redesigned Coronet pillared coupe. The inspiration—and the drivetrain—were pure Road Runner. But for the name, Dodge looked to its Scat Pack symbol and released its new model in the spring of '68 as the Super Bee.

The $3027 base price was $131 over that of the Road Runner, which used the same basic chassis. Curb weight was nearly identical, so performance was a wash. Base engine for both was the 335-bhp four-barrel 383-cid V-8 that borrowed cylinder heads, camshaft, and induction system from the 440 Magnum V-8. The 426 Hemi was the only engine

option, but at nearly $1000, it clashed with the Super Bee's budget appeal and only 125 were ordered. A Hurst-shifted four-speed manual was standard, with the three-speed TorqueFlite automatic optional.

Holding the price meant minimizing amenities, and while Super Bee borrowed the Charger's Rallye gauge layout to edge the Road Runner in instrumentation, a tachometer still cost $38 extra. Heavy duty suspension and brakes and red-line wide-oval tires were standard, though.

Low priced didn't mean low profile. Bumblebee racing strips circled the tail, and a big Super Bee emblem hovered on the rear fenders. The grille was finished in black matte and the hood held a decorative power bulge.

Dodge was proud enough to name names in Super Bee advertising: "It's the super car for the guy who doesn't want to shy away from GTOs . . . only their high prices." But finishing far behind the Road Runner in sales surely must have stung.

Specifications

1968 Dodge Super Bee

Wheelbase, in. 119.0

Weight, lbs. 3395

Production 7717

Price $3027

Engine ohv V-8

Displacement, cid 383

Fuel system 1 × 4bbl.

Compression ratio 10.0:1

Horsepower @ rpm 335 @ 5200

Torque @ rpm 425 @ 3400

Representative performance

0-60 mph, sec. 7.1

¼ mile, sec. @ mph 15.0 @ 96

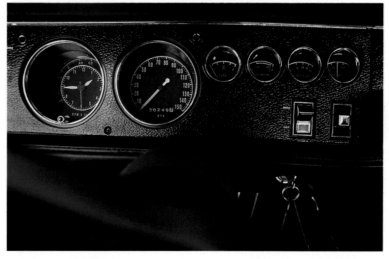

Super Bee, a midyear offshoot of the Coronet, was Dodge's response to Plymouth's Road Runner. A "stripper" pillared-coupe, its low base price included a 335-bhp 383-cid four-barrel, four-speed with Hurst Competition-Plus shifter, heavy-duty suspension, and complete instrumentation lifted from the Dodge Charger. With its tongue-in-cheek graphics, the Super Bee was a member in good standing of Dodge's performance-oriented "Scat Pack," which the automaker promoted as the "Cars with the bumblebee stripes." Of 7842 built for '68, 125 had the 426 Hemi option.

1968 Ford Mustang 428 Cobra Jet

*A*sk the most-knowledgeable Ford enthusiasts for the quickest pure-production Mustang ever and rare will be the one who doesn't name the 1968 428 Cobra Jet.

Big-block Camaros and Firebirds, and even 340-cid Darts and Barracudas, were kicking Mustang's tail on the street. Ford countered by making its 427-cid V-8 a Mustang option in early '68 models, but it was a detuned 390-bhp version of the legendary near-race 427, and its slim availability and $755 cost were downers.

Then, on April 1, 1968, Ford unreined the Cobra Jet. It was based on the staid 428 big-car engine, but had larger-valve heads, the race-brewed 427 intake manifold, and an oil-pan windage tray. It also had ram-air induction and a functional hood scoop. The scoop mated to a special air cleaner with a vacuum-actuated butterfly valve that funneled air directly into the 735-cfm Holley quad. Output was around 410 bhp, but Ford rated it at 335 bhp in an effort to calm insurance agents and con drag-strip rules-makers.

The 428 CJ was offered in Mustang fastbacks and coupes (and in Torino, Cougar, and Cyclone models) with a four-speed manual or three-speed automatic. Cobra Jet Mustangs had beefed-up front shock towers and Polyglas F70x14 tires. Four-speed cars got staggered rear shocks. Standard were 3.50:1 gears, with 3.91:1 and 4.30:1 ratios available.

CJ Mustangs came with GT-level touches, such as front fog lamps and a side "C" stripe, but the only other external clue to the armament within was the black scoop and hood stripe. The entire package cost about $500, including front disc brakes. The Equa-Loc differential ($79) and Competition Handling Package ($62) were wise extras.

With 11.5-second ETs at 120 mph, Ford's team of eight CJ Mustangs obliterated everything in their Super Stock class at the '68 NHRA Winternationals. The impact was no less forceful on the street. "The entire world will come to recognize this engine—the 428 Cobra Jet—at the pop of a hood," declared *Motor Trend*. Finally, the competition was chasing Mustang's tail.

Specifications

1968 Ford Mustang 428 Cobra Jet

Wheelbase, in. 108.0

Weight, lbs. 3620

Production 2258

Price $3600

Engine ohv V-8

Displacement, cid 428

Fuel system 1 × 4bbl.

Compression ratio 10.6:1

Horsepower @ rpm 335 @ 5400

Torque @ rpm 440 @ 3400

Representative performance

0-60 mph, sec. 5.4

¼ mile, sec. @ mph 14.01 @ 101

A landmark in Ford muscle was the mid-1968 introduction of the 428 Cobra Jet Mustang. The 428-cid Cobra Jet V-8 had a Holley quad, competition-brewed 427 V-8 heads, and ram-air induction. Ford built 2258 CJ Mustang fastbacks and 564 coupes. All had Mustang GT trim, suspension, and interior, and added a functional hood scoop marked off by a classy black stripe.

1968 Shelby
Cobra GT 500-KR

*I*f the King of the Road looked more threatening than it really was, so be it. Shelby's 1967 GT 500 had led Ford's pony car across the 400-cid threshold with a 427-cid detuned race engine and a juiced 428-cid Police Interceptor V-8. Both returned for '68. Then in April '68, Ford unveiled an even-hotter version of the 428, the Cobra Jet, and offered it in the Mustang, among other models.

At Shelby, the Cobra Jet replaced the original 428, and GT 500s gained a KR suffix, for King of the Road. (The 427 was dropped.) This was the year's second name change. Shelby's AC Cobra roadster died after '67, but he kept the name, rechristening his Mustangs the Shelby Cobra GT 500 and Shelby Cobra GT 350. (The GT 350 for '68 used Ford's new 302-cid V-8 and was rated at 250 bhp.)

The GT 500-KR's 428 had the same suspiciously low 335-bhp rating as other Cobra Jets, though some Shelby material put peak output at higher rpm. Shelby's version had diecast aluminum Cobra rocker cov-

ers, but wore the same plain painted ram-air air cleaner.

Plain did not describe the GT 500-KR. This was the first year for a Shelby convertible, and like the fastback, it dressed up the stock Mustang with its own fiberglass nose panels, fiberglass hood with working scoops and air-extraction vents, decorative bodyside intakes, and a spoil-ered tail with sequential turn signals. The fastback's roof scoops directed air to the cabin. A padded roll bar with attached inertia-reel shoulder harness, improved gauges, and woodgrain appliqués marked the otherwise stock-Mustang interior.

With its fat tires and suspension tweaks, the GT 500-KR outhandled all but pure sports cars. But it weighed more than a Cobra Jet Mustang and as a drag racer, it was no Hemi-hunter. To most street rivals, however, one look was all it took. "Oddly, the KR's vincibility doesn't matter," observed *Car Life*. "The car is so impressive, so intimidating to challengers, that there are no challengers. The KR breeds confidence bordering on arrogance."

Specifications

1968 Shelby Cobra GT 500-KR

Wheelbase, in. 108.0

Weight, lbs. 3780

Production 933

Price $4860

Engine ohv V-8

Displacement, cid 428

Fuel system 1 × 4bbl.

Compression ratio 10.6:1

Horsepower @ rpm 335 @ 5200

Torque @ rpm 440 @ 3400

Representative performance

0-60 mph, sec. 6.0

¼ mile, sec. @ mph 14.3 @ 100

Shelby's GT 500 began the '68 season with Ford's 428-cid Police Interceptor V-8. When Shelby made the midyear switch to the new 428 Cobra Jet, the GT 500 got a new suffix, KR, for King of the Road. This was the first year Shelby offered a regular-production convertible, and GT 500-KR numbers included 933 fastbacks and 318 ragtops. All had new fiberglass front and rear fascias. Scoops on the hood and on the fastback's roof functioned; the bodyside intakes did not. A tach and roll bar were added to the standard Mustang interior.

1968 Hurst/Olds

*G*ood thing George Hurst's work was as good as his promotional fervor, because he had a big appetite for attention. By the mid '60s, the former Philadelphia repair-shop owner's name was on some of drag racing's wildest exhibition cars, from the wheelstanding Hemi Under Glass to the tire-frying twin-engine Hurst Hairy Olds. And then there was Linda Vaughn, Miss Hurst Golden Shifter. . . .

But for every stunt, there was a good product, like great transmission linkages or Hurst's most-important invention, the Jaws of Life rescue tool. It was conservative Oldsmobile, however, that first put the ballyhooed Hurst name on a production car.

The division's 4-4-2 entered '68 with curvaceous new styling courtesy of GM's intermediate-car revamp. Its 400-cid V-8 had 350 bhp—360 with the new Force Air option, a factory-installed induction system that inhaled through scoops beneath the front bumper. The W-30 option returned as a blueprinted 360-bhp mill backed by a beefed-up drivetrain and cost $263.

Hurst engineer Jack "Doc" Watson had built his boss a custom '68 4-4-2. The enterprising Hurst sold Olds on the publicity value of building a limited run of similar cars for sale through key Olds dealers. Whether the Cutlass S coupes Olds shipped to an outside assembly site were already equipped with the special 390-bhp 455-cid Toronado V-8 is under debate, but all the cars did get Force Air systems and Turbo Hydra-matics with a Hurst Dual-Gate shifter.

The suspension used the best factory components, so handling was on a par with the lauded 4-4-2's. The 455 V-8 was no handicap; it actually weighed 12 pounds less than the 400. All cars were painted Toronado "Peruvian Silver" with black accent stripes and rear-deck panel.

Outstanding power, fuss-free performance, full warranty, and exclusivity came at $1161 over the sticker of a regular 4-4-2. Dealers took 3000 orders for the car, far more than could be filled. The hype was real, and the '68 Hurst/Olds marked the start of a great muscle-car friendship.

Hurst modified 451 Cutlass hardtops and 64 pillared coupes with 455-cid V-8s to create the first Hurst/Olds. They had the factory's Force Air system, which used under-bumper inlets to feed twin air-cleaner snorkels. Cars with air conditioning had 380 bhp, others had 390, but all got automatics with Hurst Dual-Gate shifters. Custom silver and black paint and wood dashboard trim were standard. Note this car's eight-track tape player.

Specifications

1968 Hurst/Olds

Wheelbase, in. 112.0

Weight, lbs. 3800

Production 451

Price $4200

Engine ohv V-8

Displacement, cid 455

Fuel system 1 × 4bbl.

Compression ratio 10.5:1

Horsepower @ rpm 390 @ 5000

Torque @ rpm 500 @ 3200

Representative performance

0-60 mph, sec. 5.4

¼ mile, sec. @ mph 13.9 @ 103

1968 Plymouth GTX

With the hot new Road Runner anchoring the lower rungs, a familiar name returned to top off Plymouth's mid-size muscle ladder. For its second season, the GTX moved to the same redesigned Belvedere platform used by the Road Runner.

In keeping with its upscale mission, the GTX featured two-door hardtop and convertible body styles; the '68 Road Runner started with a pillared coupe and didn't offer a ragtop.

Instead of adopting the 383-cid V-8 as its base engine, the GTX carried over its '67 powertrains. The 375-bhp Magnum 440-cid four-barrel was standard, with the take-no-prisoners 425-bhp 426 Hemi the sole engine option. TorqueFlite automatic, a $206 extra on the Road Runner, was standard on the GTX, and the four-speed manual was a no-cost alternative. Both cars had similar suspension upgrades and wide-oval rubber; front disc brakes and a limited-slip diff were shared options. Nonfunctional hood vents also were common to both.

While even a loaded Road Runner looked pretty plain on the outside, the GTX dressed its part with standard chrome wheel-lip moldings, tail-panel brightwork, and double side stripes. And where the Road Runner started with a fleet-grade interior, the GTX came with the well-appointed Sport Satellite cabin featuring shiny details and fake woodgrain. The differences showed in base prices: $3355 for the GTX hardtop, $3034 for the Road Runner coupe.

Die-hard racer types loved the Hemi, but just 450 GTXs were ordered with the $564 option. The 440, which wasn't offered on the Road Runner, was easier to keep in tune. And unlike the rev-hungry Hemi, the big wedge churned out a surplus of low-end torque for unparalleled response on the street.

Deficiencies mirrored those of the Road Runner—and of most other muscle intermediates: stiff ride, over-assisted power steering, and skittish handling on rough roads. But for a gentleman's supercar, the GTX was dialed in.

"As a performance car, the GTX has few equals," concluded *Car Life*. "With the 440 engine, it offers as much performance-per-dollar as anything on the market, and more than most."

GTX continued atop the line of restyled mid-size Plymouths. Like Road Runner, it was based on the two-door Belvedere, but was the only Plymouth equipped the 375-bhp 440 four-barrel. Of 18,940 GTXs built for '68, 414 hardtops and 36 convertibles got the optional 426 Hemi. TorqueFlite was standard, a four-speed was a no-cost option. The hood vents were phony. All used the upscale bucket-seat Sport Satellite interior. This car's chrome steel wheels are factory options, but the tires are incorrect.

Specifications
1968 Plymouth GTX

Wheelbase, in. 116.0

Weight, lbs. 4100

Production 17,500

Price $4100

Engine ohv V-8

Displacement, cid 440

Fuel system 1 × 4bbl.

Compression ratio 10.1:1

Horsepower @ rpm 375 @ 4600

Torque @ rpm 480 @ 3200

Representative performance

0-60 mph, sec. 6.4

¼ mile, sec. @ mph 14.3 @ 97.9

1968 Plymouth Road Runner

*M*uscle cars had evolved from mainstream models with expensive special engines to expensive special models with expensive special engines. What the youth of America needed was an inexpensive mainstream model with an inexpensive special engine. In '68, Plymouth gave it to them.

It started with a pillared coupe, the lightest and least-costly iteration of the handsome new Belvedere body. The engine was Mopar's proven 383-cid V-8, but with heads, manifolds, camshaft, valve springs, and crankcase windage tray from the big, bad 440 Magnum. With its four-barrel carb and unsilenced air cleaner, the new mill made 335 bhp.

Serious-minded standard features included a strengthened four-speed manual, 3.23:1 gears, beefed suspension with high-rate rear leaf springs, 11-inch heavy-duty drum brakes, and Polyglas F70x14s. TorqueFlite was optional. The interior was bench-seat austere and the base price was a stingy $2896.

Plymouth paid Warner Bros. $50,000 for rights to decorate the new model with the name and likeness of a cartoon bird. It was just the right touch. The Road Runner became a smash hit. Plymouth forecasted sales of 2500; buyers snapped up nearly 45,000. *Motor Trend* called it "the most brazenly pure, non-compromising super car in history... its simplicity is a welcome virtue."

Given the 383's strong feel and the car's reasonable weight, 15-second ETs were a tad disappointing. The $88 High-Performance Axle Package with its 3.55:1 Sure Grip got more out of the 383.

But low-13s were just $714 away via the lone engine option: a 425-bhp 426 Hemi. Just 1019 Road Runners got the Hemi, which came with a 3.54:1 Sure-Grip Dana 60 axle as a $139 mandatory option. Power front discs and power steering were smart extras. At midyear, a hardtop coupe was added, as was an optional underdash knob to open the otherwise-decorative hood vents.

Critics debated the wisdom of paying $17 for the cop-attracting matte-black hood treatment, and opinion divided on whether the "beep-beep" horn sounded like the cartoon bird or a delivery van. It actually was the sound of success.

Specifications

1968 Plymouth Road Runner

Wheelbase, in. 116.0

Weight, lbs. 3850

Production 28,400

Price $3500

Engine ohv V-8

Displacement, cid 383

Fuel system 1 × 4bbl.

Compression ratio 10.0:1

Horsepower @ rpm 335 @ 5200

Torque @ rpm 425 @ 3400

Representative performance

0-60 mph, sec. 7.1

¼ mile, sec. @ mph 15.0 @ 96

After the '64 Pontiac GTO, the '68 Road Runner is muscle's most-significant car. With a standard 335-bhp 383 four-barrel and few amenities, it brought performance to a wide new audience. This one has extra-cost wheels, but is otherwise a fine example of a basic bench-seat, 383 car. Total '68 production was 44,589; 383s went into 28,400 pillared coupes and 15,179 hardtops, the optional 425-bhp 426 Hemi went into 840 coupes and 179 hardtops.

1968 Pontiac Firebird 400

Pontiac may have broken late from the gate in the pony car derby, but it was quickly making up ground. Carefully considered alterations made the Firebird 400 perhaps the best all-around sporty compact of '68.

Styling was unchanged save for deletion of side vent windows and addition of federally mandated fender marker lights. Beneath the skin, Pontiac engineers continued to refine the Camaro-spec suspension forced on them by GM. Performance versions of both makes got new multiple-leaf rear springs with shock absorbers staggered fore and aft of the axle, so axle tramp in hard takeoffs was diminished. Pontiac went further to improve overall road manners with new options such as adjustable Koni shock absorbers ($42). Front disc brakes remained a $63 extra, but some 400s reportedly were equipped with new variable-assist power steering, which provided a quicker ratio yet firmer control at high speeds.

Horsepower on the standard 400-cid V-8 increased by five, to 330. Ram Air continued as the rarest and strongest engine option at about

$600 over the regular 400. It again had a hotter cam, stronger valve springs, and exclusive use of functional hood scoops. At midyear, the 335-bhp Ram Air mill was replaced by the 340-bhp Ram Air II.

A third 400 engine variation bowed for '68, and was the best blend of machismo and manners. The 400 HO, or High Output, cost about $350 over the base 400 and used free-flow exhausts and, when hooked to a four-speed, its own revised cam. It too was rated at 335 bhp, but redlined higher than the base engine and below the Ram Air. All 400s used a single four-barrel carb and came with either a three- or four-speed manual or optional three-speed automatic. The four-speed was standard on Ram Air cars.

In a 1968 *Car and Driver* comparison test, a Firebird 400 HO bested a 390-cid Javelin, a 390 Mustang and 390 Cougar, a Camaro SS 396, and a 340 Barracuda. Not only was the Poncho quickest of the bunch, but its engine was the smoothest and its handling the friendliest.

"For sheer enjoyment and confidence behind the wheel," said *Car and Driver*, "the Firebird was almost in a class by itself."

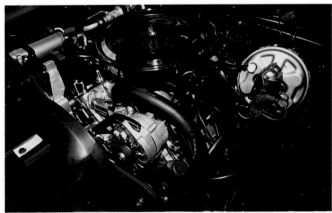

Like its Camaro cousin, Pontiac's pony lost its wing windows for '68, but changed little otherwise. Some 2087 Firebird 400s, including this Starlight Black ragtop, had the laudable new 335-bhp High-Output V-8. Its other options include Rally II wheels, Hurst-shifted close-ratio four-speed, and console with clock.

Specifications
1968 Pontiac Firebird 400 HO

Wheelbase, in. 108.1

Weight, lbs. 3700

Production 2087

Price $3950

Engine ohv V-8

Displacement, cid 400

Fuel system 1×4bbl.

Compression ratio 10.75:1

Horsepower @ rpm 335 @ 5000

Torque @ rpm 430 @ 3400

Representative performance

0-60 mph, sec. 5.5

¼ mile, sec. @ mph 14.2 @ 100

1968 Pontiac GTO

When GM redesigned its intermediates for '68, no division had a tougher act to follow than Pontiac. But talent rose to the challenge and the new GTO emerged as a brilliant blend of beauty and brawn. It sustained the styling leadership of the 1966-67 series, and its performance remained competitive against ever-tougher rivals. Best of all, its aura was intact.

"In image, performance and class, the 'Tiger' is the car to equal," said *Motor Trend* in its survey of Detroit's '68 muscle armada. "Face it," said impressed *Hot Rod* editors after their first drive in the new Goat, "this is Pontiac's era."

Gone was the pillared coupe, leaving a two-door GTO hardtop and convertible, again with the best dash layout in supercar land. Curb weights were up about 75 pounds over '67, but a wheelbase shortened from 115 inches to a nimbler 112, another year of suspension tuning, and standard G77x14 tires improved handling enough to rival that of the best GM intermediate, the Oldsmobile 4-4-2.

Nothing rivaled the GTO's new energy-absorbing Endura bumper, which was molded and color-keyed to form the car's clean new nose. Hidden headlamps also were new and were so popular that most people didn't realize they were options.

A 400-cid four-barrel V-8 remained standard. The base version gained 15 bhp, to 350, while the HO and Ram Air editions climbed to 360 bhp. Midyear, Pontiac replaced the original Ram Air engine with the Ram Air II. Improvements included new cylinder heads, forged pistons, and lighter valves. Compression was unchanged, but output rose to 366 bhp. The Ram Air induction hardware was again shipped in the trunk for installation by the dealer. All engines were available with Hurst-shifted stick or automatic, though Ram Air cars came only with 4.33:1 gears and without air conditioning.

The steering transmitted too much road shock and had too little feel, and some sheetmetal wasn't the stoutest. But in the increasingly treacherous muscle jungle, the new GTO remained one of the big cats.

The second-generation GTO's triumphant restyle included the novel energy-absorbing Endura bumper. Its bucket-seat interior remained a study in the art of muscle-car cabins. Sales were a healthy 87,684, of which 9337 hardtops and 1227 convertibles got the new 360-bhp 400-cid HO engine option. This owner installed the over-the-counter factory Ram Air system on his 400 HO V-8.

Specifications

1968 Pontiac GTO

Wheelbase, in. 112.0

Weight, lbs. 3800

Production 9337

Price $4300

Engine ohv V-8

Displacement, cid 400

Fuel system 1 × 4bbl.

Compression ratio 10.75:1

Horsepower @ rpm 360 @ 5100

Torque @ rpm 445 @ 3600

Representative performance

0-60 mph, sec. 6.4

¼ mile, sec. @ mph 14.5 @ 98

1969 AMC
Hurst SC/Rambler

*L*augh if you will, but the AMC Hurst SC/Rambler could blow the doors off some pedigreed muscle cars. Too bad AMC had to compensate for its slim advertising budget by making a billboard of the car.

Having dipped into performance with the '68 AMX and Javelin pony cars, Detroit's No. 4 automaker decided to expand into the budget-muscle arena with—don't snicker—a Rambler Rogue compact. Directed by Hurst Performance Research Inc., the project followed the simplest hot-rod canon: stuff in the biggest available V-8. In AMC's case, that was the AMX's 315-bhp 390-cid four-barrel. A Borg-Warner four-speed with a Hurst shifter and a 3.54:1 limited-slip completed the drivetrain.

Heavy-duty shocks, anti-sway bar, and anti-hop rear links fortified the suspension. E70x14 Polyglas tires and the AMX's optional heavy-duty brakes with front discs were included. Inside were reclining buckets. Instrumentation was standard Rouge with the exception of a Sun 8000-rpm tach strapped to the steering column.

The car debuted midway through the model year as the AMC SC/Rambler-Hurst; most called it the Scrambler. Only 1512 were built, and they were potent little screamers. But that exterior treatment! No one seemed to like it. A "tri-colored nickelodeon," said *Car and Driver*.

All SC/Ramblers started as appliance-white hardtops with two-tone mags, racing mirrors, blackout grille and tail panel, Hurst badging, and a real ram-air hood scoop with an upthrust snout that unfortunately recalled the nose of a hound sniffing for the scent. About 1200 Scramblers went full "Yankee Doodle," with broad red bodysides, wild hood graphics, and a fat blue dorsal stripe. The rest made do with only simple rocker-panel striping.

With ETs in the low to mid-14s, however, some unwary rivals wouldn't have to look at the whole car. "This sort of acceleration," said *Road Test*, "is going to show the Hurst emblem on the back to a few GTOs, Cobra Jets, Road Runners, and Mach 1s."

Specifications

1969 AMC Hurst SC/Rambler

Wheelbase, in. 106.0

Weight, lbs. 3300

Production 3160

Price $2998

Engine ohv V-8

Displacement, cid 390

Fuel system 1 × 4bbl.

Compression ratio 10.2:1

Horsepower @ rpm 315 @ 4600

Torque @ rpm 425 @ 3200

Representative performance

0-60 mph, sec. 6.3

¼ mile, sec. @ mph 14.3 @ 99

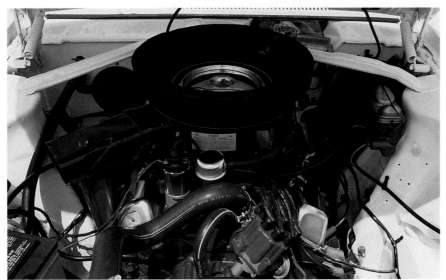

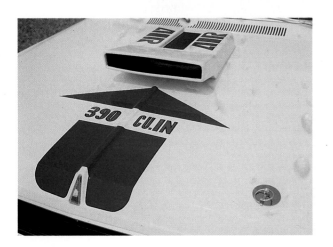

AMC took the time-honored muscle-car route of putting its biggest engine in a compact body, and with help from Hurst, created the SC/Rambler. It was a sort of supercar caricature, with an exaggerated hood scoop and lampoonish paint and graphics. But a 390-cid V-8, performance drivetrain, and light weight made it pretty quick. The car debuted in mid '69 and sold for that year only. A $61 AM radio was the sole option.

1969 Buick GS 400

GM's midsize cars entered the second year of their current styling cycle with each division maneuvering to increase its muscle profile. Chevy uncorked some special-order super Chevelles; Olds headlined Hurst editions of the 4-4-2; and Pontiac's big news was a pop-culture-inspired version of the GTO.

Buick didn't have a special model of its GS 400. But neither did it stand pat. In fact, the GS 400 got standard functional hood scoops for '69, something none of its higher-profile corporate siblings had. The "Cool Air" induction system used a twin-snorkel air cleaner with two foam muffs that sealed against the scoop openings. Buick said the system increased peak horsepower by eight percent and peak torque by six percent over the entire rpm range, though the car's base 400-cid V-8 retained the 340-bhp rating from '68.

But now, the base engine wasn't the only GS 400 mill. New for '69 were Stage 1 and Stage 2 option packages. Stage 1 boosted output to

345 bhp. It had a high-lift cam, 11.0:1 compression instead of 10.25:1, a special carburetor and fuel pump, and larger low-restriction exhausts. Positraction was included, and four-speed cars got 3.64:1 gears. The optional three-speed automatic was modified for higher shift points and used 3.42:1 cogs. The rare Stage 2 made up to 360 bhp with an even hotter cam and other assorted enhancements.

True to Buick's nature, the Stage 1 was energetic but untemperamental. Even the advertising line—"Buick builds a premium performance machine"—seemed high-toned.

"The Stage 1 engine feels like a good supercar compromise," *Motor Trend* concurred. "Power is all there for street running, especially when you put your foot in it and open all four barrels. Downshifting acceleration really puts you back in your seat. One distinct characteristic of the engine seems to be its smoother idle with a big cam. It's not nearly as rough as similar supercars with similar grind cams."

Buick's 1969 GS 400 gained standard functional hood scoops that sealed against two foam air-cleaner muffs. The standard 340-bhp 400-cid V-8 could also be treated to Stage 1 factory hop-ups good for 350 bhp, or Stage 2 upgrades, for 360. Optional bucket seats and floor shift for the extra-cost TH-400 automatic added some sportiness to the interior. Convertibles accounted for 1776 of the 8132 GS 400s built that year.

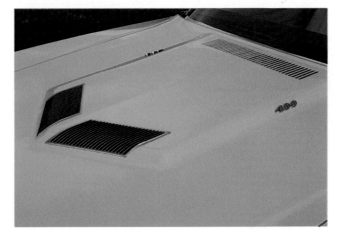

Specifications

1969 Buick GS 400 Stage 1

Wheelbase, in. 112.0

Weight, lbs. 4070

Production 1776

Price $4350

Engine ohv V-8

Displacement, cid 400

Fuel system 1 × 4bbl.

Compression ratio 11.0:1

Horsepower @ rpm 345 @ 5800

Torque @ rpm 440 @ 3200

Representative performance

0-60 mph, sec. 5.8

¼ mile, sec. @ mph 14.4 @ 97

1969 Chevrolet Camaro SS 396

*O*n occasion, Detroit comes up with a one-year wonder that strikes a chord with its audience. The '69 Camaro was like that.

A deft revamp of the original 1967-68 body shell created unique styling used for just this season. Good thing the '69s were so interesting. As it turned out, they had to be carried into the '70 model year when production problems delayed introduction of the fully redesigned next-generation Camaro.

The most-popular enthusiast Camaro was again the Super Sport, which added about $300 to a coupe or convertible and included a 300-bhp 350-cid V-8, stiff suspension, and F70x14 tires. Power front disc brakes were now part of the package, as were the nonfunctional hood ports previously exclusive to SS 396s. An extra $79 landed the new cowl-induction hood with its functional rear-facing inlet. The hidden-head-lamp Rally Sport option cost $132. The interior was updated, too, and a new $95 gauge pack put a round tach in the instrument pod and auxiliary dials on the center console.

Except for rare 427-cid specials, big-cube Camaro muscle was best expressed in the SS 396. The respected engine was back in three basic states of tune: 325 and 350 bhp, and the 375-bhp L78, which cost $316. For $711, Chevy would fit an L78 with aluminum heads. It called these L89s and rated them at 375 bhp; 311 went into Camaros.

Chevy worked to improve the behavior of the big-block Camaro's rear suspension. But the 396 had so much torque and put so many pounds over the nose—59.3-percent of an SS 396's weight was on the front axle—that the lightly loaded rear axle struggled to get the power down in hole shots. "At the mere suggestion of work, the axle leaps and hops, judders and bucks . . . " said *Road Test*. "The rear suspension is (the) weak linkage between axle and car, and it drags the 396 Camaro down to the level of just another Camaro."

Savvy street racers attacked the problem with aftermarket traction kits, which cut ETs significantly. And as time would prove, no '69 was "just another Camaro."

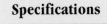

Specifications

1969 Chevrolet Camaro SS 396

Wheelbase, in. 108.1

Weight, lbs. 3790

Production 4889

Price $4000

Engine ohv V-8

Displacement, cid 396

Fuel system 1 × 4bbl.

Compression ratio 11.0:1

Horsepower @ rpm 375 @ 5600

Torque @ rpm 415 @ 4600

Representative performance

0-60 mph, sec. 6.8

¼ mile, sec. @ mph 14.7 @ 98.7

All-new sheetmetal made for a strikingly different Camaro in '69—the only year this styling was offered. More than 34,000 Camaros were outfitted in Super Sport trim; of 13,970 ordered with 396-cid V-8s, 4889 got the hot 375-bhp L78 version. L78 ragtops were extremely rare. This one eschewed the hidden-headlamp Rally Sport package, but added Rally wheels and treated its cabin to the optional Special Interior Group with a simulated woodgrain steering wheel and a Sports console that included extra gauges. The cassette tape deck shown is a later, aftermarket item.

1969 Chevrolet
Camaro Z28

*I*t wasn't the fastest, but with single-season styling and a unique combination of brake, engine, exhaust and induction options, the '69 was arguably the most desirable Z28 of all.

Adding $458 to the $2726 base price of a Camaro coupe, RPO Z28 included the F41 handling suspension with E70x15 raised-letter tires on seven-inch rims, quicker steering, and twin rally stripes. Front disc brakes were standard, and for the first time, four-wheel discs were offered. They cost $500 and just 206 sets were delivered, about half going to full race cars.

The solid-lifter 302-cid V-8 with an 850-cfm four-barrel was again exclusive to the Z28. Dyno tests at close to 400 bhp made a joke of its 290-bhp rating. Dealer-installed dual-quad options were offered even in '67, and for '69, $500 bought twin 600-cfm Holleys on a cross-ram manifold, though at no change to the 290-bhp rating. Chambered exhaust pipes—perhaps the least-restrictive exhausts Chevy ever offered—also were available.

Yet another functional option unique to '69s was the $79 cowl-induction hood. It had a valve that snapped open at 80-percent throttle to draw in cool air from the base of the windshield.

Z28s again came only with a Hurst-shifted close-ratio four-speed; 3.73:1 gears were standard, with up to 4.10:1 available. Positraction was an option. Styling could be enhanced by the Rally Sport package, which gained transparent louvers for its hidden-headlamp covers.

Handling was razor-sharp, aided by power steering that was both quick and had road feel. Four-barrel cars could turn 14.8s at 101, but the small-block's shortage of low-end torque was multiplied with the dual-quads, which fed on sky-high revs. Even dropping the clutch at 4000 rpm produced stumble off the line.

As Trans Am titles in '68 and '69 showed, the Z28 was a road-racer first, a street machine second. Drivers who understood its bare-knuckle character bought 7199 of them for '68, and sales nearly tripled for '69—a record that would stand until 1978.

Specifications

1969 Chevrolet Camaro Z28

Wheelbase, in. 108.1

Weight, lbs. 3765

Production 20,302

Price $5207

Engine ohv V-8

Displacement, cid 302

Fuel system 2 × 4bbl.

Compression ratio 11.0:1

Horsepower @ rpm 290 @ 5800

Torque @ rpm 290 @ 4200

Representative performance

0-60 mph, sec. 7.4

¼ mile, sec. @ mph 15.12 @ 94.8

The '69 edition is among the most-desirable Z28s, and this Garnet red example is a virtual checklist of its most-coveted equipment. Options include upgraded interior trim, the cross-ram dual-quad induction system for the standard solid-lifter 302, four-wheel disc brakes, and the Rally Sport package, which concealed the headlights behind hinged doors. The cowl-induction hood was optional.

1969 Yenko Camaro 427

To Ford fans, Carroll Shelby is the high-priest of performance. Chevy loyalists revere a Canonsburg, Pennsylvania, car dealer named Don Yenko. Yenko had a deserved reputation for driving, building, and selling dominating Chevrolets, starting in '65 with well-crafted super Corvairs. He advanced to installing 427-cid Corvette V-8s in '67 and '68 Camaros, performing 118 of the transplants. These $4200 ponys ran in the low 13s right off his shop floor.

Other Chevy retailers, notably Nickey in Chicago, Dana in California, and Baldwin-Motion in New York, undertook similar transplants. But Yenko Sports Cars Inc. had dealer outlets for its cars in 19 states, and that earned clout with Chevrolet. Dealer conversions were complicated, however, and came with only a limited engine warranty. So at Yenko's urging, Chevy agreed to factory-build a batch of 1969 Camaros with 427 engines, and to provide full 5-year/50,000-mile warranties. This was done under the Central Office Production Order system, which had previously been used to satisfy special requests from non-performance fleet buyers.

How many COPO Camaros were built isn't known; Yenko ordered 201, but other dealers could order them as well, and 500 or more were produced. All were basically the same: They had the iron-block and head, solid-lifter L72 427, which Chevy pegged at 425 bhp but which Yenko rated a more-realistic 450; Hurst four-speed manual or dual-gate automatic; heavy-duty 4.10:1 Posi; cowl-induction hood; heavy-duty Z28 suspension with F70x14 tires; and other go-fast goodies. The package added about $800 to a base coupe, including $490 for the engine.

Chevy delivered the standard COPO Camaros with dog-dish hubcaps and no exterior badging; not even the engine was identified as a 427. Yenko ordered his with 15-inch rally wheels, bigger front roll bar, and 140 mph-speedometer, then dressed them with "sYc" (Yenko Super Car) insignia and striping, and made available mags, gauges, headers, and other items that could push the price past $4600. As delivered, Yenko Camaros turned effortless mid-13s. Most were fitted with headers and slicks, even for street work, and in this form recorded 11.94-second ETs at 114 mph.

Specifications

1969 Yenko Camaro 427

Wheelbase, in. 108.1

Weight, lbs. 3500

Production 201

Price $4500

Engine ohv V-8

Displacement, cid 427

Fuel system 1 × 4bbl.

Compression ratio 11.0:1

Horsepower @ rpm 425 @ 5600

Torque @ rpm 460 @ 4000

Representative performance

0-60 mph, sec. 5.4

¼ mile, sec. @ mph 13.5 @ 102

Pennsylvania Chevy dealer and bow tie performance maven Don Yenko applied his special touch to 201 '69 Camaros equipped via the Central Office Production Order system with 427-cid V-8s. Yenko didn't modify the L72 big-block, but he did rate it at a realistic 450 bhp and would fit Doug Thorely headers. His cars came with 15-inch wheels and the Camaro spoiler package, and most got unique "Yenko Super Car" stripes and emblems. All COPO Camaros had a Hurst-shifted four-speed or Dual-Gate automatic. Yenkos got additional gauges, including a Stewart Warner tach.

1969 Chevrolet
Camaro ZL1

*F*irst. Most powerful. Quickest. Only one Chevy combines it all: the ZL1 Camaro. It went a step beyond the 427 Yenko and even the mighty L88 Corvette, to where few production cars tread.

Drawing a bead on NHRA Super Stock drag classes, Chevy performance guru Vince Piggins authorized the factory to fit a batch of '69 Camaros with a version of the 427-cid V-8 used by the all-conquering Can-Am Chaparral. This actually was another of Piggins' Central Office Production Order projects, and like the COPO Chevelles and Camaros being built for '69, the ZL1 was technically a Camaro option package.

The cars began as 396-cid/375-bhp Super Sports with the F41 suspension. Engine and SS trim were deleted, and the cars were equipped essentially as other 427 COPO Camaros, with cowl-induction hood, front disc brakes, a choice of heavy-duty four-speeds or Turbo Hydra-matic, and a 4:10.1 Posi in the strongest axle Chevy could muster. But instead of the iron-block and head L72 427, these Camaros got a 427 called the ZL1. It was similar in design to the most-potent iteration of the alu-

minum-head L88, but it was the first production Chevy engine to also have an aluminum block. It shared the L88's 430-bhp factory rating, but actually had over 500 bhp—making it likely the most powerful engine Chevy ever offered to the public. And it weighed just 500 pounds—about the same as Chevy's 327-cid V-8.

The entire car carried the full 5-year/50,000-mile warranty and was fully street-legal. With the factory's stock dual exhausts and tires, it turned low 13s; headers, slicks, and tuning got it into the 11.6s at 122 mph. Chevy never built a quicker production car.

All this came at a price: $4160 for the ZL1 engine alone, pushing the car's sticker to a stratospheric $7200. Chevy needed to build 50 to satisfy the NHRA, and actually built 69. About 20 ZL1s went into organized drag racing, turning low 10s to set several Super Stock records. Well-heeled individuals bought others, but the high price took a toll: At least 12 engines were removed and sold separately, and about 30 unsold cars were returned to Chevy. It took until the early '70s to sell them off.

Specifications

1969 Chevrolet Camaro ZL1

Wheelbase, in. 108.1

Weight, lbs. 3300

Production 69

Price $7200

Engine ohv V-8

Displacement, cid 427

Fuel system 1 × 4bbl.

Compression ratio 12.0:1

Horsepower @ rpm 430 @ 5200

Torque @ rpm 450 @ 4400

Representative performance

0-60 mph, sec. 5.3

¼ mile, sec. @ mph 13.16 @ 110

At the apex of Chevy muscle was the '69 ZL1 Camaro. Sober outside except for the cowl-induction hood, and unadorned inside (not even a factory tach), its engine bay packed pure terror. Its all-aluminum 427-cid V-8 had a competition pedigree and was known as the ZL1. This engine also went into two production Corvettes.

1969 Chevrolet
Chevelle SS 396

Although the SS 396 Chevelle was muscle for the common man, set up the right way, its performance was distinctly uncommon.

After a year as a separate model, the SS 396 was made a $348 option package for '69. That widened its availability from the Malibu sport coupe and convertible, to the Chevelle 300-series hardtop and pillared coupe (it also was offered on the open-bed El Camino). All Chevelles got minor styling changes, including new taillamps. SS 396s looked cleaner than ever. The power-bulge hood was still just for show, but more-prominent "SS 396" badging inside and out and standard five-spoke mag wheels burnished the image.

Decidedly not for show was the L78 version of the 396-cid V-8. Costing $253 more than the base 325-bhp 396 and $132 over the 350-bhp L34, the solid-lifter L78 was again rated at 375 bhp, but its punch down low and big lungs at high rpm made it feel stronger.

Car and Driver's Patrick Bedard sang the L78's praises in his 1990 "warrior's list" of muscle cars: "There was no single genius part, no hemi head or tunnel port that you could point to and say, 'Yep, that's what makes this the baddest motor in town.' All the pieces just worked together as if they were on commission."

Muscle was entering its heyday and Chevy not only sold a record 86,307 SS 396s in '69, but more than 9000, an all-time high, were ordered with the L78. An estimated 400 buyers shelled out an additional $395 for the L89 option, which fit the L78 with weight-saving aluminum heads.

The three-speed Turbo Hydra-matic was now the only automatic available on an SS 396, and was the first strong enough to handle the L78. The L78 was also the only mill offered with the infamous Rock Crusher four-speed. The SS 396 now included power front discs, with the F41 suspension and free-flow chambered exhausts among new options.

Continued traction problems and a sloppy four-speed linkage gave box-stock examples deceptively modest ETs. Some comfort was gained in the knowledge that few muscle cars responded as well to simple modifications, showing that common doesn't always mean average.

Specifications

1969 Chevrolet Chevelle SS 396

Wheelbase, in. 112.0

Weight, lbs. 3700

Production 400

Price $3750

Engine ohv V-8

Displacement, cid 396

Fuel system 1 × 4bbl.

Compression ratio 11.0:1

Horsepower @ rpm 375 @ 5600

Torque @ rpm 415 @ 3600

Representative performance

0-60 mph, sec. 6.5

¼ mile, sec. @ mph 14.5 @ 101

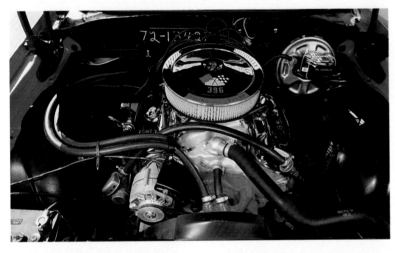

Making the SS 396 an option package for '69 expanded availability from dressy Malibus and open-bed El Caminos to more-basic Chevelle 300 Deluxe pillared-coupes like this one. Super Sport standing earned it mag wheels and an SS steering wheel; L89 aluminum cylinder heads on its 375-bhp 396 earned it respect. The four-speed shifter in an otherwise Spartan cabin enhanced its street-stormer status. Late in the '69 model year, Chevy's 396-cid engine was bored out to 402 cid, but the automaker retained the "396" title and badging to capitalize on its name recognition.

1969 Chevrolet
Chevelle COPO 427

At the opposite end of the COPO spectrum from Yenko's striped and badged Chevelles were those delivered just as Chevy built them. These supercars spoke softly, but carried a very big stick.

All COPO Chevelles were cut from the same basic cloth. Their reason for being was GM's ban on engines over 400 cid in midsize cars. Hotbloods within Chevy itched to circumvent the rule. And with a handful of muscle-hungry dealers egging them on, Vince Piggins, Chevy's performance-products manager, found a way. He used the Central Office Production Order system, which normally filled special-equipment fleet orders, to factory-equip a run of Chevelles with L72 427-cid V-8s.

As in the COPO Camaro, the solid-lifter iron-block-and-head L72 used an aluminum manifold and an 800-cfm Holley four-barrel. Chevy rated it at 425 bhp, but in calculating the car's stock drag class, the NHRA claimed a truer 450 bhp. Chevelle's strongest regular four-speed or the Rock Crusher manual were offered, as was a fortified Turbo Hydra-matic. The strengthened 12-bolt Positraction axle had 4.10:1 cogs

and the suspension was heavy-duty. Front discs—standard on Super Sport Chevelles—were a mandatory $64 option on COPO cars.

In fact, none of the 323 COPO Chevelles built were Super Sports. Instead, they were base coupes with a COPO option package that cost about $860, including $533 for the L72. Yenko put his trademark dress-ups on the 99 he ordered. But the balance that went to other dealers for individual sale looked deceptively docile.

From the SS they borrowed a black grille and tail panel, hood bulges, side stripes, and chrome exhaust tips. However, there was no performance ID on the body. The emblem-free L72 could pass for an aluminum-manifold 396. And the cabin was plain Malibu, though a few SS steering wheels were fitted. Even the standard rally wheels were similar to those on the base Malibu, though they were in reality 15-inch units.

The cid-ceiling would be lifted for '70, so COPO Chevelles were built for 1969 only. But these were among the most feared muscle cars of any day. And they didn't need any badges.

Specifications

1969 Chevrolet Chevelle COPO 427

Wheelbase, in. 112.0

Weight, lbs. 3800

Production 323

Price $3800

Engine ohv V-8

Displacement, cid 427

Fuel system 1 × 4bbl.

Compression ratio 11.0:1

Horsepower @ rpm 425 @ 5600

Torque @ rpm 460 @ 4000

Representative performance

0-60 mph, sec. 5.1

¼ mile, sec. @ mph 13.3 @ 108

This is how a COPO 427 Chevelle looked like as delivered from the factory. Unlike Yenko's versions, its styling was low-key. There were no exterior performance badges and nothing on the engine identified it as the formidable 427-cid L72 V-8. They had regular Malibu bucket-seat interiors, though some got Super Sport steering wheels. This Le Mans blue example is among the estimated 96 COPO Chevelles equipped with automatic transmission. Chevy built these limited-edition special-order supercars for 1969 only.

1969 Chevrolet
Nova SS 396

*S*ome street racers weren't attention seekers. They got their kicks by humbling flashy, high-buck muscle cars, shutting them down in an ambush of speed and stealth. The Nova SS 396 seemed ideal for such duty. But looks can be deceiving.

Chevy had redesigned its compact for '68, but the look was still pretty tame. The chassis design, however, was shared with the Camaro, so big-blocks finally fit. Sure enough, the 396-cid V-8 appeared as a Super Sport option partway through '68. For '69, the 396 was back in 350-bhp tune and—for those who knew how to play the order form—as the 375-bhp L78.

This was the hoodlum Nova. Building one began with the SS package. It added $280 to the $2405 base price of a Nova pillared coupe and included a 300-bhp 350-cid V-8, special suspension, red stripe F70x14s, and power front discs. Replacing the 350 with the L78 cost another $500, but even with the $184 close-ratio four-speed, $43 limited-slip diff, and excellent $84 fast-ratio power steering, the price was an enticing $3500 or so.

SS badges, black-accented grille and tail, and simulated hood air intakes marked the exterior, but nothing shouted supercar. Still, all stealthiness seemed to dissolve with the L78. What the "396" numerals on the fender suggested, the racket of solid lifters and the ominous rumble from dual exhausts confirmed.

"The junior Chevy with the senior engine . . . is an instantly recognized and feared street cleaner," reported *Car and Driver*. "The 396 Chevy II sure wasn't the invisible sleeper we had expected, but it was every bit as wild as we hoped."

Not only did the SS 396 stuff big power into a 3400-pound package, it put just 55 percent of its heft on the front axle, a favorable weight balance few muscle cars could match. Even so, torque and tire slip conspired to quell bite off the line. Cheater slicks solved the problem. True, they may have given away the Nova SS 396's true mission, but its cover was blown the moment the L78 fired up, anyway.

Specifications

1969 Chevrolet Nova SS 396

Wheelbase, in. 111.0

Weight, lbs. 3400

Production 5262

Price $3500

Engine ohv V-8

Displacement, cid 396

Fuel system 1 × 4bbl.

Compression ratio 11.0:1

Horsepower @ rpm 375 @ 5600

Torque @ rpm 415 @ 3600

Representative performance

0-60 mph, sec. 5.9

¼ mile, sec. @ mph 14.5 @ 101

With clean but unassuming styling, an SS 396 Nova would seem to have been the perfect sleeper. But not in 375-bhp L78 form: The clatter of solid lifters and the rumble from its dual exhausts attracted too many eyes to those "396" badges. Of 7209 SS 396 Novas built for '69, 5262, including this one, got the L78.

1969 Yenko Nova 427

While Chrysler gave its blessing to installations of 440-cid V-8s and even 426 Hemis in compact Darts and Barracudas, Chevy wanted little to do with the mating of a 427-cid V-8 and a Nova. Don Yenko, of course, jumped at the chance.

"That was the wildest thing we ever did," the renowned Chevy dealer and hot-car builder told *Muscle Car Review* in 1987.

Unlike COPO Camaros and Chevelles, the 427 Nova was not a factory-installation. Instead, Yenko ordered Super Sport Novas equipped with the 396-cid/375-bhp V-8, then his shop transplanted the 425-bhp L72 427. As with his COPO Camaro and Chevelle, Yenko rated the Nova Super Car at 450 bhp. It used the same close-ratio Muncie four-speed with Hurst linkage or a Turbo Hydra-matic with Hurst Dual-Gate shifter, and a heavy-duty 4.10:1 Posi axle. The Novas had 14x7-inch wheels, compared to 15x7s on the Yenko Camaro and Chevelle. But the usual Yenko-supplied headers, Atlas mags, and tachometer were available.

Dressed out in Yenko striping, 427/Yenko badges, and "sYc" headrests, these Novas made no attempt to disguise their true character. They were produced for 1968 and '69 only, in numbers well short of the COPO Camaros and Chevelles. But with less weight than either—even less than a 427 Corvette—and surprisingly good front-rear weight distribution, the L72 Nova was likely the fastest automobile Don Yenko ever offered.

"The car was a beast, it was almost lethal," Yenko himself admitted in the '87 interview. "In retrospect, this probably wasn't the safest car in the world . . . it was not for amateurs. With the proper tires and the right driver, we had it clocked at 0-60 mph in under four seconds. I really was skirting the edge of product liability. . . ."

Don Yenko was 54 when he died in the March 1987 crash of his private airplane. His enthusiasm lives on in cars celebrated equally for their spectacular performance and for their link to a very special figure in the history of muscle.

Dropping the L72 427 V-8 into Chevy's compact made for a wild Nova that even Don Yenko feared. It had the same hyper-performance powertrain as L72 COPO Camaros and Chevelles, but less mass and better weight distribution than either. And it was even faster. Just 37 were built. This one has proper "sYc" trim, but not the SS 396-type hood ports seen on the other Yenko Novas.

Specifications
1969 Yenko Nova 427

Wheelbase, in. 111.0

Weight, lbs. 3300

Production 37

Price $4000

Engine ohv V-8

Displacement, cid 427

Fuel system 1 × 4bbl.

Compression ratio 11.0:1

Horsepower @ rpm 425 @ 5600

Torque @ rpm 460 @ 4000

Representative performance

0-60 mph, sec. 4.7

¼ mile, sec. @ mph 13.2 @ 103

1969 Dodge Charger 500 & Daytona
1970 Plymouth Road Runner Superbird

"Win on Sunday, Sell on Monday" was a Detroit mantra in the 1960s. It was truest of NASCAR performance, and the war between Chrysler and Ford for superspeedway supremacy produced the most outlandish cars of the muscle age.

Dodge's '68 Charger was an aerodynamic washout on 190-mph high-banked ovals. To reduce drag, Mopar engineers plugged the nose cavity with a flush-mounted Coronet grille. They quelled lift by flush-mounting a rear window over the recessed backlight. The new racer was called the Charger 500 and 392 similarly modified production cars were built to qualify it for NASCAR. They were basically Charger R/Ts with Charger 500 metalwork. Racing Charger 500s captured 18 NASCAR victories in '69. Trouble was, Ford's droop-nosed aero warriors won 30. Back to the wind tunnel went Mopar engineers. They emerged with the Charger Daytona. Instead of a flush nose, it wore a pointed 18-inch extension that reduced drag and enhanced downforce. It retained the

Charger 500's flush backlight, but eliminated rear-end lift by mounting a horizonal tail stabilizer on tall vertical extensions. Again, street-going versions had to be built and 503 were. Except for the wild nose and tail, they were essentially 1969-model Charger R/Ts.

The Daytona debuted during the '69 NASCAR season and was faster than the Charger 500, but it came too late to beat Ford. It returned for the '70 season accompanied by the Superbird, a similar Plymouth design based on the Road Runner. Together they recaptured for Chrysler the NASCAR championship. (Plymouth built 1935 roadgoing Superbirds as 1970 models.) Competition editions of all three cars used 426-cid race Hemis. Customer versions had either the 440 or the Hemi. Charger 500s were as quick as like-powered '68 Chargers, but the winged cars weighed as much as 300 pounds more than regular Chargers and Road Runners. Acceleration and handling were correspondingly affected, but their real impact was as the muscle car taken to its magnificent extreme.

The skyscraper wing was the chief visual cue of both cars. Like the Superbird's, Daytona's was made of aluminum with an adjustable horizontal member. Offset by a color-contrasting tape stripe, the Dodge's wing was shorter and less-angled than the Plymouth's, though neither did any aerodynamic good below about 90 mph.

Nosecones of both cars were made of metal with fiberglass tubs for the pop-up headlamps. Shape and grille location differed slightly. Fendertop vents were decorative, but on race cars, they covered gaps cut for tire clearance.

Both cars had a flush-mounted rear window, but the Superbird's needed more work. The surgery was hidden by a vinyl top and finished off with aero-disruptive trim pieces that made race versions three mph slower than Daytonas. Plymouth used a body-color wing with unique decals. With the 440 engine, Superbird's price was $4298 and Daytona's was $4000. Both sold slowly and some dealers cut off the wings to please buyers.

The original Charger 500 was based on a '68 model but was marketed as a 1969 with a base price of $3860. (A '70 version was sold, but it was not the race-based design.) Among production cars, Hemi engines went into 32 Charger 500s, 70 Dodge Charger Daytonas, and 135 Superbirds. The balance of the Dodges had four-barrel 440s. Superbirds could get the 440 four-barrel or the triple two-barrel.

1969 Dodge Coronet R/T

With all the hoopla surrounding the arrival of the Super Bee Six Pack and the continued popularity of the Charger, a Dodge original seemed lost in the shuffle. The Coronet R/T was the first Dodge to unify traditional muscle elements under one nameplate back in '67. Sales topped 10,000 for its first two years, but would slide to 7200 for '69, and to 2600 for 1970—the car's swan-song season.

But quantity is not quality, of course, and Dodge continued to fine-tune its gentleman's muscle car for '69. Grille and taillamps were revised and 15-inch cast-aluminum road wheels were optional in place of the standard 14-inchers.

The 375-bhp 440 Magnum four-barrel was again standard. Just 97 hardtops and 10 convertibles were ordered with the sole engine option, the 425-bhp 426 Hemi. A Ramcharger fresh-air induction package that added two sizable hood scoops was a new option with the 440 and was standard with the Hemi, but it didn't alter power ratings.

Dodge had formed the Scat Pack to standardize marketing of its performance-car offerings, and now even the R/T's axle ratios were being organized into unified component packages. For example, the drag-oriented Track-Pak grouped a 3.54:1 Dana axle, Sure-Grip differential, dual-point distributor, heavy-duty four-speed with Hurst shifter, and heavy-duty cooling system. Other packages emphasized handling or highway cruising.

On the subject of axle ratios, *Car Life* observed that the 440 Magnum V-8 and three-speed TorqueFlite automatic combination in its Coronet R/T test car was so responsive that the standard 3.23:1 cog could have been replaced with a more-economical 2.76:1 axle ratio with little loss of acceleration.

"The 440's brute torque makes high revving completely unnecessary," the magazine said. "Shift points up to 5500 rpm were tried, but 5000 rpm gave the best performance."

Dodge had simplified its hot intermediate to produce the budget-muscle Super Bee, and used its platform for the glamour-muscle Charger. In between was the Coronet R/T, a muscle-car original holding—and occasionally dominating—the middle ground.

Specifications

1969 Dodge Coronet R/T

Wheelbase, in. 117.0

Weight, lbs. 4100

Production 6600

Price $4200

Engine ohv V-8

Displacement, cid 440

Fuel system 1 × 4bbl.

Compression ratio 10.0:1

Horsepower @ rpm 375 @ 4600

Torque @ rpm 480 @ 3200

Representative performance

0-60 mph, sec. 6.5

¼ mile, sec. @ mph 14.6 @ 97

Coronet R/T returned with a revised grille and taillamps, but without change to its wasp-waist, Coke-bottle contours. This one has the standard four-barrel 440 Magnum V-8 and TorqueFlite automatic, plus optional 15-inch polished wheels, but not the new Ramcharger Air Induction System, which added dual hood scoops.

1969 Dodge Dart GTS

*I*f Dodge had a car to rival the energetic small-block Chevy, it was the Dart with the eager, free-revving 340-cid V-8. Underrated at 275-bhp, a 340 Dart could crack off easy mid-14-second ETs, to the embarrassment of many a big-block supercar. But this was the '60s. Balance and finesse were not the order of the day. If the 340 was good, a 383-cid Dart would be even better. Right? Not necessarily, as it turned out.

Dart had been redesigned for '67, and the two-door hardtop enjoyed pleasing, if undramatic, proportions. The 340 and 383 came on board for '68. The 340 was standard in the showcase GTSport trim level, which included bumblebee tail stripes to mark its membership in the new Dodge Scat Pack collection of performance cars.

Optional in the GTS was the 383 four-barrel. It was rated at a realistic 300 bhp. The 340, however, actually produced 300 bhp or more, and weighed 90 pounds less than the 383. Where the GTS's heavy-duty suspension was a fine match for the 340, allowing power to flow smoothly to the pavement, the 383 upset this balance. Traction off the line was poor, and ETs were no quicker.

For '69, the 383 got the full Road Runner/Super Bee treatment and horsepower climbed to 330. As in '68, Dodge made some changes to the GTS's suspension when the 383 was ordered, increasing the diameter of the front torsion bars and front sway bar. But the same heavy-duty six-leaf rear springs and E70x14 tires were retained. Transmissions were shared, as well: either a heavy-duty four-speed or high-upshift TorqueFlite, both with 3.23:1 gears standard and 3.55:1 or 3.91:1 available with the optional Sure Grip diff.

A sensitive foot on the gas pedal still was required to get a 383 Dart off the line without wasting precious seconds simply smoking the tires. But once hooked up, the '69 car's extra power seemed finally to make this marriage work. It still wasn't the best all-around engine in this application, but what would the '60s have been without a little excess?

Specifications

1969 Dodge Dart GTS 383

Wheelbase, in. 111.0

Weight, lbs. 3500

Production NA

Price $3800

Engine ohv V-8

Displacement, cid 383

Fuel system 1 × 4bbl.

Compression ratio 10.0:1

Horsepower @ rpm 330 @ 5200

Torque @ rpm 410 @ 3600

Representative performance

0-60 mph, sec. 6.0

¼ mile, sec. @ mph 14.4 @ 99

Dart GTS production totaled 5717 hardtops and 360 convertibles for '69, most equipped with the tough 340-cid four-barrel. That one, underrated at 270 bhp, was a darling of the critics. The optional 330-bhp 383 V-8 wasn't. It had 70 lb-ft more torque than the 340, enough to overwhelm the rear tires in hole shots, and its weight spoiled the GTS's balanced road manners. Either could be ordered with manual or automatic, and bucket seats were optional. Note the separate shoulder belts strung from the headliner. Bee badges and stripes marked the GTS as a member of Dodge's Scat Pack.

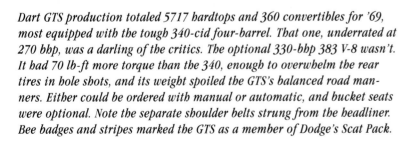

1969 Dodge
Super Bee Six Pack

*I*n mid 1969, Chrysler engineers used some good-old hot-rodding to create one of the muscle era's most intoxicating cars.

They took Mopar's fine 375-bhp 440-cid Magnum V-8 and treated it to the time-honored hop-up of more carburetion, replacing the single Carter quad with three Holley two-barrels on an Edelbrock Hi-Riser manifold. Normal driving ran the engine on the center carb; punching it opened the two outboard Holleys and delivered an astounding 1375-cfm charge. Hemi valve springs, a hotter cam, magnafluxed connecting rods, and other fortifications helped boost output to 390 bhp.

A Hurst-shifted four-speed and a 9¾-inch Dana Sure-Grip diff with 4.10:1 gears were standard. TorqueFlite was optional, but disc brakes, air conditioning, and cruise control were not allowed.

Dodge's home for the new mill was the econo-muscle Coronet Super Bee, which again came with a 383-cid V-8 or the 426 Hemi. In honor of the tri-carb setup, the newcomer was called the Super Bee Six Pack, a name broadcast on the sides of one of the wilder hoods in muscledom.

Its scoop lacked a filter or valve to keep out foreign elements—though it did have rain drain tubes. With its matte-black finish and NASCAR tie-down pins, the fiberglass lift-off hood said this car meant business, a message reinforced by standard steel wheels unadorned except for chrome lug nuts. (The engine and hood also were offered in the '69 Plymouth Road Runner as the "440+6".)

Dodge's 440 Six Pack cost $463, about $500 less than a Hemi. No Mopar mill was as all-out fast as the Hemi. But the 440 could hang with one until 70 mph or so, and the deep-breathing Six Pack added a near-Hemi high end. "The result was a torque motor that would rev, too, a fearsome street cleaner," wrote *Car and Driver*'s Patrick Bedard in his 1990 muscle retrospective.

With their Hemi-grade suspension, Six Pack Super Bees were surprisingly good handlers. That outragous hood did bait cops, and made every oil check a two-person job. So what? Considering its price and performance, this Six Pack was a small-deposit, high-return steal.

Specifications

1969 Dodge Coronet Super Bee Six Pack

Wheelbase, in. 117.0

Weight, lbs. 4100

Production 1907

Price $4300

Engine ohv V-8

Displacement, cid 440

Fuel system 3 × 2bbl.

Compression ratio 10.5:1

Horsepower @ rpm 390 @ 4700

Torque @ rpm 490 @ 3200

Representative performance

0-60 mph, sec. 6.3

¼ mile, sec. @ mph 13.8 @ 104.2

Muscle got no meaner than the Super Bee Six Pack. Based on the econo-performance Coronet-derived Super Bee of '68, it got its name from the three Holley two-barrels atop its 440-cid V-8. The massive scoop was functional and the chrome pins really held down the lift-off fiberglass hood. It came without wheel covers, just chrome lug nuts. This one has optional bucket seats and console, plus the hot ticket for street work, the TorqueFlite automatic.

1969 Ford
Fairlane Cobra 428

*F*ord jumped on the budget-muscle bandwagon in '69 with a midsize model that was a little out of character for the brand: it performed. The subject was a dressed-down Fairlane hardtop or SportsRoof fastback with the grille blacked out and minimal exterior ornamentation; about the only clue to the car's true nature were small Cobra snake emblems and "428" badges.

They signified the 428-cid Cobra Jet V-8, which was standard. The $3200 base price also included a four-speed manual, with automatic a mere $37 option. Estimates put the Cobra Jet's true output at around 400 bhp, though Ford rated it at 335. The optional Ram Air induction system cost $133 and used a functional hood scoop to feed an air-cleaner breather valve that opened under heavy throttle. These CJ-R engines retained the 335-bhp rating, but were stronger than the standard mill, and turned high-13s at 102 mph.

Like the '68 econo-racer Mopars that launched the segment, Cobra stuck to basics. A "competition" suspension with staggered rear shocks, F70x14 tires, and hood-lock pins were standard. Power steering ($100) and power front discs ($65) were extras. Limited slip was a $63 option, but available ratios included 4.30:1 gears in a bulletproof Detroit Locker, which required an engine oil cooler. Interior was bench-seat plain; bucket seats with console added $169, an 8000-rpm tach, $48.

Like the mainstream intermediate on which it was based, the Cobra had a benign feel on the road, with predictable handling and numb power steering. But unlike most Fords, it flew.

"The 428 had . . . a lethargic way about it: it wasn't zingy like a Chevy," recalled Patrick Bedard for a 1990 *Car and Driver* retrospective. "But it had earth-mover torque, and it stayed in tune—exactly what street racers needed. It was good with an automatic, too: just punch it and hang on. Which meant that every CJ was a threat no matter what kind of yahoo was in the chair."

Specifications

1969 Ford Fairlane Cobra 428

Wheelbase, in. 116.0

Weight, lbs. 3900

Production NA

Price $3900

Engine ohv V-8

Displacement, cid 428

Fuel system 1 × 4bbl.

Compression ratio 10.6:1

Horsepower @ rpm 335 @ 5200

Torque @ rpm 440 @ 3400

Representative performance

0-60 mph, sec. 5.5

¼ mile, sec. @ mph 14.4 @ 101

Inspired by low-buck midsize muscle rivals, Ford uncoiled the Fairlane Cobra for '69. It came standard with the brawny 428-cid Cobra Jet V-8. This is the base version; the Ram Air option added a hood scoop that mated to an air-cleaner breather setup. Both were rated at 335 bhp. Fairlane Cobras also came as SportsRoof fastbacks, but notchbacks were about 60 pounds lighter. Options on this four-speed car include buckets, console, and tachometer.

1969 Ford Talladega & Mercury Cyclone Spoiler II
1970 Ford King Cobra

*F*ord spent a lot of the 1960s and early 1970s watching the tail-lights of quicker Mopar and GM muscle rivals. But in NASCAR, the forces from Dearborn were consistent front-runners. For '69, their new machine was so hot that even superstar Richard Petty defected from Plymouth to drive it. It was called the Talladega, after NASCAR's newest superspeedway. This was Ford's answer to Dodge's wind-tunnel wonder, the Charger 500, and as required of Dodge, Ford built street versions to qualify it for racing.

The Talladega was based on the 1969 Fairlane Cobra SportsRoof, but with some vital aerodynamic differences. The nose was tapered and stretched by five inches, and a flush-mounted grille replaced the recessed production one. The front bumper was actually a Fairlane rear bumper narrowed to fit. And the rocker panels were raised one inch so the race cars could be lowered correspondingly without violating NASCAR's ride-height requirements.

NASCAR versions ran Ford's 427-cid V-8, then switched to the Boss 429. Street Talladegas used the 335-bhp 428 Cobra Jet with a column-shift automatic. None had ram air, but all got a Drag Pack oil cooler. Cobra-issue bench-seat interiors were used.

Mercury quickly copied the formula, producing the Cyclone Spoiler II. With unique striping and a rear spoiler, street versions were flashier than Talladegas, though Mercury made the 290-bhp 351 V-8 standard and the 428 CJ an option.

Ford's aero warriors trounced the Charger 500, winning 30 races, including eight by Petty, and bringing Ford the '69 NASCAR title. When the King Cobra version of the redesigned '70 Torino disappointed in testing, the '69 Talladegas and Spoiler IIs were retained for NASCAR's 1970 season. Petty had been lured back to Plymouth by its radical Superbird, and the title returned to Chrysler. But Ford had produced a real winner, and by happy necessity, unique members of the muscle fraternity.

They looked similar, but Spoiler II's nose was longer and slightly lower than Talladega's for less aero drag and a higher top speed. Both used a Fairlane rear bumper recut to fit and put 1959 Ford truck turn signals behind the grille. Base price was about $3800 for the Mercury, $3700 for the Ford.

Ford built 745 Talladegas, all in Wimbledon White, Royal Maroon, or Presidential Blue. Mercury built 353 similar Cyclone Spoiler IIs in a variety of colors, including blue-and-white Dan Gurney replica models sold in western states and red-and-white Cale Yarborough specials for the east. Street versions were offered for 1969 only. Racing counterparts ran in both the '69 and '70 NASCAR seasons.

Would-be successor to the '69 Talladega was the King Cobra. Based on the redesigned 1970 Torino fastback, its radically tapered nose produced enough downforce to lighten the tail and make the cars unstable at speed. Three prototypes were built, but none were raced. A proposed Mercury version also was stillborn.

The "Cyclone Spoiler" name also appeared on some regular-nose Mercury Cyclones for 1969, as did Gurney and Yarborough livery, but only aero-nose cars are genuine Cyclone Spoiler IIs.

1969 Ford
Mustang Mach 1 428 Cobra Jet

*F*ord's fight to shed its also-ran image got a boost when the Mach 1 moved into the starting gate. Here was a Mustang that looked the part of a modern muscle pony, and with the 428 Cobra Jet, it ran like one.

Mustang was restyled for '69, gaining 3.8-inches of body length—all ahead of the front wheels—and about 140 pounds of curb weight. The flowing lines looked right in new Mach 1 livery. This was the mainstream performance version. It came standard with a 351-cid V-8, but star of the stable was the optional 428-cid Cobra Jet. Essentially the same V-8 that put Ford muscle on the map in the 1968½ Cobra Jet Mustang, it came in three states of tune for '69. The base version without Ram Air cost $224; $133 more bought the fresh-air induction system, which this year used a new "shaker" hood in which a scoop mounted to the air cleaner protruded through a hole in the hood and vibrated ominously with the engine.

A third version triggered by the $155 Drag-Pack option was the 428 Super Cobra Jet Ram Air. It used the shaker scoop, plus a modified crankshaft and stronger connecting rods for better high-rpm durability, as well as an engine oil cooler that decreased lubricant temperature by 30 degrees. The Drag Pack came with limited-slip 3.91:1 or 4.30:1 cogs and excluded air conditioning. All versions used a four-speed or Ford's improved SelectShift automatic. And all were underrated at 335 bhp. But the Cobra Jet's most-pertinent product was torque, enough to send the F40x14s up in a haze of Polyglas. With 3.91:1 gearing, even the automatic broke 'em lose at each full-throttle upshift. Great for grins, bad for ETs. The root of the problem was a 59-percent-front weight bias, an imbalance that contributed to sloppy handling, as well.

But this was the Mustang Ford fans had waited for—cheaper than a Boss 429, less temperamental than a Boss 302, and a force anywhere fast cars gathered.

Specifications

1969 Ford Mustang Mach 1
428 Super Cobra Jet

Wheelbase, in. 108.0

Weight, lbs. 3600

Production NA

Price $4100

Engine ohv V-8

Displacement, cid 428

Fuel system 1 × 4bbl.

Compression ratio 10.6:1

Horsepower @ rpm 335 @ 5200

Torque @ rpm 440 @ 3400

Representative performance

0-60 mph, sec. 5.7

¼ mile, sec. @ mph 13.9 @ 103

Mach 1 debuted for '69, looking racy with a standard matte-black hood and simulated body-side air intakes, plus optional spoilers and window slats. Standard buckets, three-spoke wheel with "rim-blow" horn, and fake wood made for a sporty cabin. Top engine was the 428-cid Cobra Jet, here with the extra-cost ram-air shaker hood scoop. The Drag Pack option makes this one a Super Cobra Jet, the strongest volume-production Mustang street racer ever.

1969 Ford
Mustang Boss 429

*M*uscle fans thought this would be the Mustang to finally rival the best of the Corvettes. They were disappointed when it wasn't. But Ford never intended the Boss 429 as a street dominator, or as any kind of drag-racing threat. This gap between expectation and intent dimmed the glow of an extraordinary car.

The Boss 429 was born of Ford's need to qualify 500 examples of its new racing engine for NASCAR. But instead of putting production units in the midsize Torinos it ran in stock-car racing, Ford offered the engines in its restyled '69 Mustang fastback. It was a serious mill: four-bolt mains, a forged steel crankshaft, and big-port, staggered-valve aluminum heads with crescent-shaped combustion chambers. A 735-cfm Holley four-barrel with ram-air, an aluminum high-riser, and header-type exhaust manifolds completed the engine, which retailed for $1200. Mandatory options included a four-speed ($254) and a 3.91:1 Traction-Lok ($64). An oil cooler, trunk-mounted battery, beefed suspension with front and rear stabilizer bars, Polyglas F60x15s, quicker power steering, and power front discs rounded out the functional hardware. Boss 429s used Mustang's plushest interior decor and an 8000-rpm tach. They were refreshingly clean outside, with simple decals, black hood scoop, front spoiler, and Magnum 500 wheels. Air conditioning and automatic transmission were forbidden. This was the costliest non-Shelby Mustang, and part of the expense was a reworked front suspension to fit the big semi-hemi 429. The surprising upside was a wider front track and improved geometry that, with the husky tires, gave the Boss 429 fine handling. But who wanted handling?

The superspeedway-bound 429 thrived on high revs—bad news for standing-start acceleration. Moreover, the initial batch had incorrect valve springs and stopped winding at 4500 rpm, not the correct 6000. Even with such hop-ups as Hurst linkage, traction bars, high-performance cam, and rejetted carb, quarter-mile performance fell short of other big-block specialty cars. Ford built 1356 Boss 429 Mustangs and two Cougars for '69 and '70 before ending its factory racing program and retiring a car whose promise and purpose never really meshed.

Specifications

1969 Ford Mustang Boss 429

Wheelbase, in. 108.0

Weight, lbs. 3870

Production 857

Price $4900

Engine ohv V-8

Displacement, cid 429

Fuel system 1 × 4bbl.

Compression ratio 10.5:1

Horsepower @ rpm 375 @ 5200

Torque @ rpm 450 @ 3400

Representative performance

0-60 mph, sec. 6.8

¼ mile, sec. @ mph 14.0 @ 103

The enigmatic Mustang Boss 429 didn't deliver on its performance potential. The problem was that its semi-hemi 429-cid V-8 was a high-rev NASCAR engine, not a drag mill. On the plus side was a refreshing lack of gimmickry. The big scoop was functional, a four-speed was mandatory, and reworked suspension gave it good handling.

1969 Mercury
Cougar Eliminator

*C*ougar played the suave big brother to the rambunctious Mustang, but given the right motivation, the cat had claws.

Mercury introduced its sporty coupe in 1967 as a luxury-touring alternative to the pony-car herd. It had mature styling and upscale interior appointments, and was built on a Mustang chassis stretched by three inches to provide a longer, ride-enhancing wheelbase.

Mercury in these years was deeply involved in racing. It backed a variety of record-setting Comet and Cougar drag specials, as well as NASCAR-winning Cyclones. Its street image was tamer, though not for lack of trying. Cougar contributed with the '68 GT-E, which like the Mustang, opened the year with an available 390-bhp 427-cid V-8, then switched to the 428 Cobra Jet.

Cougar's performance profile was raised in April '69 with introduction of the new Eliminator package. Taking its cue from such rivals as Z28 and SS Camaros, as well as Ford's own Boss 302 and Mach 1 Mus-

tangs, Eliminator offered a range of engines, from the Trans Am-inspired solid-lifter 302 to the 428 Cobra Jet.

In all-out acceleration, the 290-bhp 302 was overmatched by the Cougar's weight, but the 428 Cobra Jet apparently benefitted from the relatively generous wheelbase. Grip was slightly better off the line than in the shorter Mustang, and ETs were every bit as good. Like Mustang, Eliminator offered the 428 with and without Ram Air, as well as in Drag Pak guise with an oil cooler and a 4.30:1 Detroit Locker. Eliminator didn't use the shaker hood; its standard scoop was functional only when Ram Air was ordered. A blacked-out grille, side stripe, and front and rear spoilers enhanced the look, and Mercury offered Eliminator in a palette of "high-impact" blue, orange, and yellow exterior colors.

More impact could be obtained over dealer parts counters, which offered not only headers and dual quads, but such exotic hop-ups as deep-sump oil pans and quadruple-carb Weber setups. From Mercury!

Cougar received its first restyle for '69 and Mercury answered the Boss 302 and Mach 1 Mustangs with the striped-and-spoilered Eliminator. This one has the base 428 Cobra Jet V-8 without ram air, so its hood scoop is merely decorative, but the four-speed with Hurst T-handle shifter is a highly functional feature.

Specifications

1969 Mercury Cougar Eliminator

Wheelbase, in. 111.0

Weight, lbs. 3780

Production NA

Price $4300

Engine ohv V-8

Displacement, cid 428

Fuel system 1 × 4bbl.

Compression ratio 10.6:1

Horsepower @ rpm 335 @ 5200

Torque @ rpm 440 @ 3400

Representative performance

0-60 mph, sec. 5.6

¼ mile, sec. @ mph 14.1 @ 103

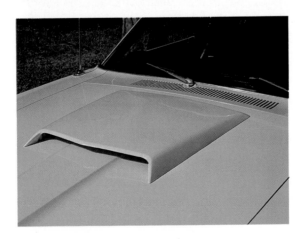

1969 Hurst/Olds

As muscle raced into the wacky late '60s, the idea of a mad scientist conjuring up ever-more-potent 4-4-2s seemed almost reasonable, and Olds advertising was rife with the image of Dr. Oldsmobile in his baggy lab coat and silent-movie mustache. In a sense, there really was such a fellow: Jack "Doc" Watson, head of research for Hurst Performance Products.

Olds was the automaker most closely associated with Hurst, which, under Watson's supervision, had produced the mighty '68 Hurst/Olds 4-4-2. Olds in fact recognized Watson's contribution to its cause by naming the ultimate 4-4-2 performance package the W-30.

The 4-4-2 itself was back with few changes for '69. Its 400-cid V-8 had 350 bhp with manual transmission and 325 with automatic. The blueprinted W-30 version returned, while the new W-32 package combined the 350-bhp variant with automatic transmission. The Force-Air option again earned a 360-bhp rating with the four-speed.

Also returning was the Hurst/Olds, but no longer was it remotely low-key in silver and black. Bold "Firefrost Gold" striping now accented

its white paint. On the hood was a flamboyant dual-snout scoop more efficient at feeding the engine than the under-bumper Force-Air inlets on other 4-4-2s. And the decklid held an enormous air foil that furnished 15 pounds of downforce at 60 mph, 64 pounds at 120 mph.

The Hurst/Olds again used the 455-cid V-8 with W-30 heads, cam, distributor, and Force-Air induction. This engine, called the W-46, was slightly detuned from '68, losing 10 bhp. A performance-modified Turbo Hydra-matic with console-shifted Hurst Dual-Gate was mandatory. Heavy-duty suspension, power front discs, and Polyglas F60x15s on special seven-inch wheels were standard. Hurst badging and imported English racing mirrors touched up the exterior, custom headrests dressed up the cabin, and air conditioning was optional.

Hurst built a couple of '69 H/O convertibles to go with the hardtops, but total production was under 1000. The Hurst/Olds would next appear as a luxury-oriented '72 Cutlass, so the fast and flashy '69s closed out its pure-muscle period on a high note, just as Drs. Oldsmobile and Watson would have prescribed.

Specifications

1969 Hurst/Olds

Wheelbase, in. 112.0

Weight, lbs. 3870

Production 912

Price $4180

Engine ohv V-8

Displacement, cid 455

Fuel system 1 × 4bbl.

Compression ratio 10.5:1

Horsepower @ rpm 380 @ 5000

Torque @ rpm 500 @ 3200

Representative performance

0-60 mph, sec. 5.9

¼ mile, sec. @ mph 14.03 @ 101

The Hurst/Olds was renewed for '69 with new styling that included a prominent rear spoiler and a florid dual-snout hood scoop that actually was more effective than Oldsmobile's standard under-bumper intakes. The standard powertrain again consisted of a hot 455-cid V-8 and an automatic with Hurst's Dual-Gate shifter.

1969 Plymouth 'Cuda 440

*P*lymouth committed itself to Barracuda performance hook, line, and, unfortunately, sinker, for 1969.

It coined the 'Cuda name to identify a new enthusiast package for fastback and hardtop models with the 340- or 383-cid engines, but the baddest 'Cuda of all came in on a wave that crested midyear. Feeling pressure from rival big-block pony cars, Plymouth cooperated with Hurst/Campbell to shoehorn Mopar's 375-bhp 440-cid four-barrel V-8 into a batch of 'Cuda fastbacks and coupes.

On the positive side, Plymouth now had bragging rights to the largest-displacement pony car of the day. And the 440 Magnum sure did get the ETs down, sometimes into the high 13s.

But there were problems. It took Plymouth two years to find room under the 383 Barracuda's hood for a power-steering unit. It finally provided one for '69, but with arrival of the 440, the engine bay was once again too crowded to allow the steering-assist hardware. With 57 per-cent of the 'Cuda 440's weight over the front tires, that was a major blow to low-speed maneuverability.

Neither did the 440 leave space for the booster that energized the front disc brakes standard on other 'Cudas. So the 440 made do with drums all around, to the detriment of stopping distances and control. Finally, Mopar engineers feared a four-speed manual transmission would encourage speed shifts and destroy the 440 car's rear end, so 440 'Cudas came only with TorqueFlite automatic.

It was difficult to get the tires to bite off the line in drag-racing starts, and the TorqueFlite—here lifted from Plymouth's family cars—didn't upshift with a racer's crispness. On the open road, the 440 'Cuda's abundant power reserves furnished effortless passing, and its steering and braking shortcomings were minimized. It clearly wasn't a complete success, but the lessons of '69 were invaluable, and big-block 'Cudas would soon resurface with a vengeance.

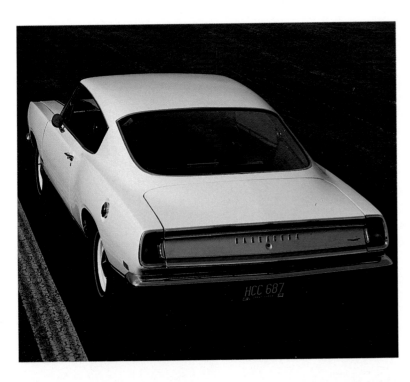

Specifications

1969 Plymouth 'Cuda 440

Wheelbase, in. 108.0

Weight, lbs. 3740

Production 340

Price $3900

Engine ohv V-8

Displacement, cid 440

Fuel system 1 × 4bbl.

Compression ratio 10.1:1

Horsepower @ rpm 375 @ 4600

Torque @ rpm 480 @ 3200

Representative performance

0-60 mph, sec. 5.6

¼ mile, sec. @ mph 14.01 @ 104

Plymouth could claim the largest-displacement pony car up to that time, but the 440-cid 'Cuda it introduced in mid '69 was a victim of too much enthusiasm and too little engineering. The 375-bhp four-barrel's surplus of torque overwhelmed the rear tires and the engine's size prevented Plymouth from fitting the nose-heavy car with power steering or power brakes. All had TorqueFlite transmission. The 'Cuda's hood scoops were not functional.

1969 Plymouth Road Runner Hemi

"What is it like on the street? Breathtaking. The Hemi Road Runner has more pure mechanical presence than any other American automobile... It has an impatient, surging idle that causes the whole car to quiver... Open everything in the two four-barrel Carters [and] the exhaust explodes like Krakatoa and the wailing howl of surprised air being sucked into the intakes turns heads for blocks. Baby, you know you're in *the presence*."

That was *Car and Driver* after comparing the '69 Hemi Road Runner against five other econo-racers that, in just one year, had sprung up to imitate Plymouth's budget-muscle blockbuster. Such breathless prose wasn't rare; anyone who drove a Hemi Road Runner seemed similarly affected.

With the Road Runner accounting for 35 percent of its midsize-car sales, Plymouth didn't tamper much with the winning formula as set out in the '68 original. A convertible joined the hardtop and pillared coupe,

the grille and taillamps were revised, and the bird insignia were now in full color. A center console, front buckets, and power windows were added to the options list.

The 335-bhp 383-cid four-barrel returned as standard, with the 425-bhp 426-cid Hemi again the top engine option. Midyear, buyers got a third choice, the same triple-two-barrel 440-cid V-8 that debuted in the '69 Dodge Super Bee. Here it was called the "440+6" and it came with the big-scoop, lift-off fiberglass hood, Hurst shifter, and 4.10:1 Sure-Grip. The 390-bhp 440+6 provided Hemi-style acceleration for about half the price. But Hemi-style does not mean Hemi excitement. *Motor Trend* knew that after swaggering up California's car-crazy Sunset Strip in a blood-red '69.

"The rough, hard idle swells up and out from under the car, ricochets off other cars, and rams into the ears of the driver, the spectators. You think twice about a 383 Road Runner, but a hemi only once—and let it pass."

Specifications

1969 Plymouth Road Runner Hemi

Wheelbase, in. 116.0

Weight, lbs. 3940

Production 356

Price $4000

Engine ohv V-8

Displacement, cid 426

Fuel system 2 × 4bbl.

Compression ratio 10.25:1

Horsepower @ rpm 425 @ 5000

Torque @ rpm 490 @ 4000

Representative performance

0-60 mph, sec. 5.3

¼ mile, sec. @ mph 13.55 @ 105

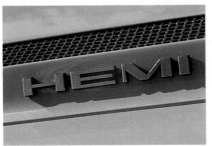

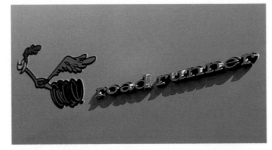

Few supercars were as savage as a Hemi Road Runner. The 426-cid V-8's dual quads breathed through newly functional Air Grabber hood vents, which were standard with the Hemi and optional with the base 383 mill. The Hemi cost $813 and went into 422 Road Runner hardtops, 356 pillared coupes, and 10 convertibles for '69. Bucket seats are among this sano four-speed's few options. Bird decals were now in full color.

1969 Pontiac
Firebird Trans Am

*O*ther than the Corvette, only one American high-performance car has remained in continuous production from its inception. That would have been hard to foresee in March 1969 when the Trans Am quietly slipped into Pontiac's lineup.

Officially titled the Trans Am Performance and Appearance Package, the $725 option was launched with little fanfare and no advertising and was ordered on just 689 Firebird coupes and eight convertibles. Its name came from the popular Trans American racing series, though the car never actually competed in Trans Am racing.

Its base engine was the Firebird 400 HO's 335-bhp 400-cid V-8, but with standard Ram Air induction. It came to be called the Ram Air III. The only alternative was the Ram Air IV version. Ordered on 55 Trans Am coupes and all eight ragtops, Ram Air IV had a longer-duration cam and 345 bhp. The base mill came with a three-speed and 3.55:1 gears, the Ram Air IV with a four-speed and 3.90:1 cogs, and both were available with automatic. A heavy-duty suspension with one-inch front stabilizer bar, Polyglas F70x14s on seven-inch rims, and special high-effort variable ratio power steering were standard.

All Trans Ams were Polar White with blue racing stripes, tail panel, and decals. The hood, a Trans Am exclusive, had functional air inlets that could be closed by the driver. Rear-facing fiberglass fender scoops covered fist-sized holes designed to vent the engine bay. A 60-inch air foil spanned the rear deck. The interior was basic Firebird, though an optional rally cluster added a 160-mph speedometer and 8000-rpm tach. Buyers also could order an $85 hood-mounted rev counter.

Acceleration was similar to Firebird's with comparable powertrains, but the Trans Am did handle. "We were safely passing chains of cars, eight, nine, ten at a whack…and not having to brake for the corner, but carving the turns at high speed," said *Sports Car Graphic* after a mountain-road sortie. It took Trans Am just three years to dethrone the GTO as Pontiac's most-popular performance offering. Its beginnings may have been humble, but the car would never be.

Specifications

1969 Pontiac Trans Am Ram Air IV

Wheelbase, in. 108.1

Weight, lbs. 3700

Production 55

Price $3950

Engine ohv V-8

Displacement, cid 400

Fuel system 1 × 4bbl.

Compression ratio 10.75:1

Horsepower @ rpm 345 @ 5400

Torque @ rpm 430 @ 3700

Representative performance

0-60 mph, sec. 6.3

¼ mile, sec. @ mph 14.1 @ 101

It debuted during 1969 as an unsung option package, but Trans Am would become one of Pontiac's most significant performance cars. To the Firebird it added a functional twin-scoop hood, rear spoiler, open fender vents, and a unique white and blue paint scheme. Standard was the 335-bhp Ram Air 400. This is one of 55 Trans Am coupes fitted with the 345-bhp Ram Air IV upgrade. Buckets, console, and specially tuned steering and suspension were included.

1969 Pontiac GTO Judge

*I*n most circumstances, a judge commands respect. But society in 1969 was increasingly irreverent toward establishment figures, and "Here comes da judge!" quickly went from a sardonic catch phrase on TV's *Laugh-In* to a staple of the American lexicon.

In naming the newest GTO incarnation "The Judge," Pontiac seemed to be saying: "This car has authority, but like the Road Runner and its ilk, it doesn't take itself too seriously." Abundantly powerful V-8s secured the first part of the message; op-art graphics and bright primary colors brought home the second.

As originally conceived, The Judge was to be an econo-muscle Goat, maybe a pillared coupe in a single color, with rubber floor mats and only the hottest performance equipment. The Judge that debuted in December 1968 wasn't so severe, being instead a $332 option package for the GTO hardtop or convertible. But it included a host of features that cost far more when ordered individually.

Standard was the 366-bhp Ram Air III evolution of the GTO's 400-cid V-8. An underdash knob now closed its hood scoops in wet weather.

Pontiac trimmed a few bucks from the base price by fitting a three-speed manual with Hurst T-handle shifter (and by deleting trim rings from the standard Rally II wheels), but all Judges had the regular firm GTO suspension and wide-tread Polyglas G70x14s.

Another $390 landed the new Ram Air IV with its radical cam and underrated 370 bhp. Restless at idle, weak below 3000 rpm, this edition of the 400 was a pain to drive on the street and a task to launch at the strip, but it was a weapon in the hands of a skilled driver. A close-ratio four-speed ($195) or automatic ($227), Posi ($63), front discs ($64), power steering ($100), and hood-mounted tach ($63) filled out the well-appointed Judge.

No somber black robes for this jurist, however. A rear-deck spoiler, blackout grille, and Judge decals decorated the body, though the cabin was standard GTO except for Judge badges. To kill any budget-muscle pretence, every regular GTO option was available, including hidden headlamps. The Judge performed no differently than similarly equipped Goats. It just did it with less reverence.

Specifications

1969 Pontiac GTO Judge

Wheelbase, in. 112.0

Weight, lbs. 4000

Production 6725

Price $4440

Engine ohv V-8

Displacement, cid 400

Fuel system 1 × 4bbl.

Compression ratio 10.75:1

Horsepower @ rpm 370 @ 5500

Torque @ rpm 445 @ 3900

Representative performance

0-60 mph, sec. 6.2

¼ mile, sec. @ mph 14.4 @ 98

Pontiac created The Judge by stirring GTO's hottest performance extras into a single $332 package and slapping on the pop-culture cues. Blacked-out grille (hidden headlamps optional), rear air foil, and 366-bhp Ram Air 400 were standard. This Orbit Orange hardtop has the 370-bhp Ram Air IV option. Interiors were stock GTO except for Judge badging. Note the Ram Air control knob beneath the steering column. Judge production for '69 was 6725 hardtops and 108 convertibles.

1970 AMC AMX

AMC was never shy about asserting that its AMX was a genuine sports car. It did have two seats and a wheelbase one inch shorter than a Corvette's. But it also was clearly derived from the Javelin pony car, with shared mechanicals, seats, and dashboard. To purists who debated whether even the 'Vette was a true sports car, a shortened Javelin wasn't worth discussing.

To most Americans, of course, the fact that the AMX wasn't an MG was an advantage. That meant it was reasonably comfortable, had lots of luggage space, and most importantly, could be equipped with a big, powerful V-8 engine.

After bowing midway through the '68 model year, the AMX was largely unaltered for '69, though a Hurst shifter did replace its inferior factory linkage. Changes were more substantial for '70.

Standard in place of a 225-bhp 290-cid V-8 was a new 290-bhp 360. The optional 390 V-8 gained 10 bhp, to 325. The restyled hood carried a scoop that was made functional when the new Ram Air option was ordered. A 390 with Ram Air was rated at 340 bhp. AMC also moved the parking/turn-signal lamps to the grille, creating holes in the bumper that it said cooled the front brakes. Actually, the ducts were too far from the binders to do much good. More effective was a revised front suspension that further improved the already-sharp handling.

Optimally set up with the $384 "Go" package, which included E70x14 tires, front disc brakes, super heavy duty suspension, limited slip diff, Ram Air, and improved engine cooling, a 390 AMX was reasonably quick in the quarter and highly competent in the corners. It was a rewarding combination, and so rare in a car from Detroit, that some testers were not about to quibble over the sports-car label.

"For the doubters we can testify once again that the AMX feels like a sports car, drives like a sports car, handles like a sports car and therefore in our book (and that of the Sports Car Club of America) it is a sports car," said *Road Test* magazine.

But this, the best AMX, was also the last true AMX. For '71, the proud AMX lost its identity as a short-wheelbase two-seater and reverted to a decor option for the redesigned and horribly bloated four-seat Javelin.

AMX got a mild facelift and a larger standard V-8 in its last season as a two-seater. This one has the top 390-cid four-barrel and the optional "Go" package, which included a new ram-air induction system that boosted output to 340 bhp. AMC claimed the openings in the front bumper accepted brake-cooling air. The sporty dash gained an 8000-rpm tach this year. The racing-stripe option was not ordered on this AMX, but Big Bad Green paint was.

Specifications

1970 AMC AMX

Wheelbase, in. 97.0

Weight, lbs. 3475

Production 4116

Price $4300

Engine ohv V-8

Displacement, cid 390

Fuel system 1 × 4bbl.

Compression ratio 10.0:1

Horsepower @ rpm 340 @ 5100

Torque @ rpm 430 @ 3600

Representative performance

0-60 mph, sec. 6.4

¼ mile, sec. @ mph 14.6 @ 98

1970 AMC Rebel "Machine"

*T*here exists in the American Motors archives a photo of a most sinister-looking muscle car. It's a black midsize coupe with authoritative black wheels and fat tires. No stripes, no scoops, no spoilers. Its body rakes forward in an aggressive, street-fighting stance. On the fender is a decal. It shows two gears chewing out the name of this macho prototype: "The Machine."

The photo is dated June 1968, and the car is a '69 Rebel. AMC's high-performance sedan efforts for '69 were focussed on the Rogue-based Hurst SC/Rambler, a brashly decorated compact as overstated as the black Rebel concept was understated. The SC/Rambler didn't survive into '70, but The Machine did. It was not, however, the malevolent rebel promised by the prototype, but a red, white, and blue jukebox of a car, clearly in the spirit of the SC/Rambler. "You have to say this for American Motors," observed *Road Test* magazine, "when they get their teeth into an idea they pursue it with a vengeance."

Luckily, The Machine was a pretty good performer. Like the

SC/Scrambler, it used the AMX's ram-air 390-cid V-8, newly souped to 340 bhp. In its journey from concept to reality, The Machine gained a big hood scoop that served the engine via a vacuum-controlled butterfly valve. A Hurst-shifted four-speed was mandatory and came with a 3.54:1 axle. AMC's limited-slip diff was a $43 option, with a genuine Detroit Locker and ratios up to 5.00:1 available.

The Machine was one of Detroit's most stiffly sprung muscle cars. Its extra-heavy-duty suspension included firm station wagon rear springs, which elevated the tail and helped account for the raked look. With E60x15 tires, cornering ability was top-notch, but rear-axle juddering off the line prevented the willing, lightweight V-8 from propelling the car into the low-14-second range.

The Machine turned out to be a one-year-only model, and after building the first 1000 or so, AMC began offering it sans stripes and in any color. It still wasn't the menacing machine of that '69 photo, but buyers could at least get the steak without quite so much sizzle.

Specifications

1970 AMC Rebel "Machine"

Wheelbase, in. 114.0

Weight, lbs. 3800

Production 2326

Price $3500

Engine ohv V-8

Displacement, cid 390

Fuel system 1 × 4bbl.

Compression ratio 10.0:1

Horsepower @ rpm 340 @ 5100

Torque @ rpm 430 @ 3600

Representative performance

0-60 mph, sec. 6.8

¼ mile, sec. @ mph 14.4 @ 99

AMC entered the midsize-muscle field with the Rebel-based '70 Machine. Early ones got a cartoonish, multi-color paint scheme, but subsequent Machines could be ordered in more-traditional hues. All got a Hurst-shifted four-speed, a 390-cid four-barrel, and a new Ram Air system that employed a vacuum-controlled hood scoop. A tachometer was integrated into a raised fairing on the scoop in front of the driver.

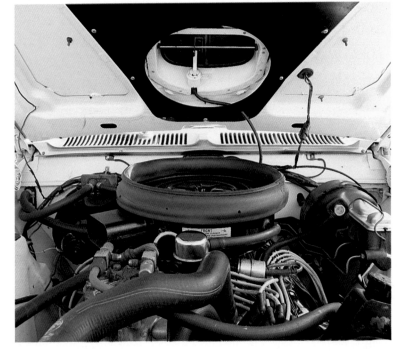

1970 Buick GSX

*G*eneral Motors surrendered itself to temptation in 1970 and lifted its 400-cid limit on intermediate cars. That unleashed some of the quickest automobiles ever to come out of Detroit and helped make this the pinnacle year for American muscle.

At the forefront of the rush to power was none other than Buick. Its performance offering was again based on the midsize Skylark, which got fresh styling that added two inches of body length on an unchanged wheelbase for '70. Replacing the GS 400 and its 400-cid V-8 was the GS 455, named for its new 455-cid V-8. The new mill offered not only advantages of displacement, but had bigger valves, better heads, and a hotter camshaft. It was rated at 350 bhp. Its prodigious 510 lb-ft of torque (at a subterranean 2800 rpm) was exceeded among production cars only by Cadillac's 474- and 500-cid V-8s. Standard on GS models were functional hood scoops that mated to dual air-cleaner intakes.

For the really power hungry, Buick offered the 455 Stage I performance package. Its tweaks included a hotter cam, even larger valves

with stronger springs, ported heads, and revised carburetor jetting. Torque was unchanged, and Buick slyly put horsepower at 360, but most testers said it was over 400. A bargain at just $199, the Stage I package included a Positraction 3.64:1 axle and performance modifications to the available three- and four-speed manuals and the automatic.

During the model year, Buick unveiled the ultimate expression of its ultimate supercar, the GSX. It added $1196 to the GS 455 and came in either Apollo White or Saturn Yellow set off by unique stripes and spoilers. A hood-mounted tach, Hurst-shifted four-speed, Polyglas G60x15s on seven-inch-wide wheels, front discs, and heavy-duty suspension were included. Of 687 GSXs built, 488 were ordered with the Stage 1 upgrade, which cost $113 on a GSX.

A 13.38-second pass at 105.5 mph prompted *Motor Trend* to crown the GS 455 Stage 1 "the quickest American production car we had ever tested." Most other magazines were in the high 13s. Any way you cut it, Buick had earned its place on muscle's all-time, all-star team.

Buick's restyled Skylark hosted the GS 455, so named for its new 455-cid V-8. Stage 1 upgrades gave it 360 bhp. The midyear GSX option elevated the GS 455's profile with an exclusive package of aero aids and graphics, creating one of the muscle era's great cars. Functional hood scoops fed standard ram air induction; note the hood-mounted tach.

Specifications
1970 Buick GSX Stage 1

Wheelbase, in. 112.0

Weight, lbs. 4000

Production 687

Price $5100

Engine ohv V-8

Displacement, cid 455

Fuel system 1 × 4bbl.

Compression ratio 10.5:1

Horsepower @ rpm 360 @ 4600

Torque @ rpm 510 @ 2800

Representative performance

0-60 mph, sec. 6.5

¼ mile, sec. @ mph 13.8 @ 101

1970 Chevrolet Camaro Z28

*T*he '67 was the first one and a sentimental favorite. A '69 dual-carb, disc-brake Rally Sport car might be the most desirable. But the 1970 edition was simply the best all-around Z28 of all.

Camaro kept its 108-inch wheelbase this year, but otherwise underwent wholesale change with a new coupe body that was an instant classic. The Z28 returned as a $573 package, the heart of which was a new engine. Trans Am racing now allowed destroking to achieve 305 cid, so the Z28 appropriated the Corvette's 350-cid LT1 V-8 as its sole powerplant. A timeless small block, the LT1 had solid lifters, a hot cam, big valves, aluminum pistons, 11.0:1 compression, and a 780-cfm Holley four-barrel. It was rated at 370 bhp in the 'Vette and 360 in the Z28.

A $206 Hurst-shifted Muncie four-speed and $44 Positraction 3.73:1 gears (with 4.10:1 available) were mandatory extras, and there was now enough low-end torque for Chevy to offer the Z28's first automatic-transmission option. Suspension advances made all '70 Camaros good handlers and the Z28, with firmer underpinnings and sticky Polyglas

F60x15s, was a world-class road car.

Hood and decklid striping, black grille, and seven-inch-wide mag-type steel wheels with polished lugs were part of the package. A rear spoiler was standard, but the air-induction hood was dropped. As before, the Z28 could be combined with the Rally Sport package, which this year went for $169 and included a unique nose treatment with a soft Endura grille surround and chrome bumperettes. Instrument positioning was improved, though a tach was part of the optional $84 gauge group.

The Z28 had matured. If it had lost some of its predecessors' juvenile zeal, it surpassed them in acceleration, balance, and refinement. *Car and Driver* called the '70 "an automobile of uncommon merit . . . a car of brilliant performance. . . ."

After pocketing Trans Am titles in '68 and '69, race Z28s finished poorly in '70, while showroom versions would lose horsepower after this year, beginning a long performance decline. The incomparable '70, then, was an apt exclamation point to the Z28's muscle years.

Specifications

1970 Chevrolet Camaro Z28

Wheelbase, in. 108.1

Weight, lbs. 3850

Production 8733

Price $4200

Engine ohv V-8

Displacement, cid 350

Fuel system 1 × 4bbl.

Compression ratio 11.0:1

Horsepower @ rpm 360 @ 6000

Torque @ rpm 380 @ 4000

Representative performance

0-60 mph, sec. 6.1

¼ mile, sec. @ mph 14.4 @ 99.1

Camaro's classic 1970 re-design was the foundation for the finest Z28 of the muscle era. Racing stripes and a rear spoiler were standard, but the cowl-induction hood was dropped. The new Z28 engine was Corvette's exhilarating solid-lifter 350-cid four-barrel, here rated at 360 bhp. (These are non-stock headers.) This Hugger Orange four-speed has the woodgrain-appliqué Sport Interior option, but not the extra-cost Rally Sport package.

1970 Chevrolet
Chevelle SS 454

*T*he age of muscle peaked in 1970 and Chevelle was there to herald its ascent. When GM lifted its displacement ban on midsize cars, Pontiac, Olds, and Buick responded with 455-cid mills with up to 370 bhp. Chevy's retort was a 454-cid V-8 that *started* at 360 bhp and ended at a barbaric 450. This was muscle's summit.

The wrapper was a restyled Chevelle that again presented the Super Sport as an option package for hardtops and convertibles. As the SS 396, it cost $446 and came with a 350-bhp 402-cid V-8, power front discs, F41 suspension, Polyglas F70x14s, and a domed hood. Fat dorsal stripes were optional, but were included with the new $147 cowl-induction hood, which had a flapper near the base of the windshield that opened at full throttle to feed air to the engine.

The new SS 454 package cost $503 and included a 360-bhp hydraulic-lifter 454 called the LS5. Then there was the LS6. This was the take-no-prisoners 454, with a 800-cfm Holley four-barrel on an alu-

minum manifold, 11.25:1 compression, solid lifters, four-bolt mains, forged steel crank and connecting rods, forged aluminum pistons, and deep-groove accessory pullies. No production engine ever had a higher factory horsepower rating. With mandatory options—including either the Rock Crusher four-speed or special Turbo 400 automatic—total cost for an LS6 was more than $1000. Axles ranged from 3.31:1 to 4.10:1, with Positraction a $42 extra.

The SS Chevelle had a handsome new dash, and on the road, exhibited far more poise than its weight and size would suggest. But the LS6 made it a superstar. Sub-14-second ETs at over 100 mph were routine.

But the LS6's thunder also seemed to signal an approaching storm, one that would dampen muscle forever. Testers sensed it. "Without even raising the specters of insurance and social justice," said *Car Life* after an LS6 experience, "it's fair to say that the Supercar as we know it may have gone as far as it's going."

Specifications

1970 Chevrolet Chevelle SS 454 LS6

Wheelbase, in. 112.0

Weight, lbs. 4000

Production 4475

Price $4930

Engine ohv V-8

Displacement, cid 454

Fuel system 1 × 4bbl.

Compression ratio 11.25:1

Horsepower @ rpm 450 @ 5600

Torque @ rpm 500 @ 3600

Representative performance

0-60 mph, sec. 6.1

¼ mile, sec. @ mph 13.7 @ 103

The 1970 Super Sport Chevelle with the solid-lifter LS6 454-cid V-8 was a tyrannical muscle car with an unsurpassed 450-bhp factory rating. It had a restyled body and shared its new gauge cluster with the Monte Carlo. Options on this four-speed car include bucket seats and console. It also has the new cowl-induction hood, which drew air from the base of the windshield via a vacuum-controlled flapper. Of 62,372 Super Sport Chevelles and El Caminos built for '70, 4298 had the LS5 454 and 4475 had the LS6. America would not see their likes again.

1970 Dodge
Challenger R/T 440 Six Pack

*I*t took Chrysler six years to develop a true pony car, and by the time the 1970 Dodge Challenger was introduced, it was hard to do anything really new with the formula. Offering an astonishing range of engine choices, from a docile slant six to the earth-shaking Hemi, was Dodge's way of getting attention.

Challenger used the same unibody platform as Plymouth's new Barracuda, but its wheelbase was two inches longer to provide slightly more rear-seat room. It was sold in hardtop and convertible form, with performance versions wearing the familiar R/T label. Standard R/T power came from the 335-bhp 383. Two 440s were offered, the four-barrel Magnum with 375 bhp and the tri-carb Six Pack with 390. The 425-bhp 426 Hemi cost $1228 with required heavy-duty equipment.

The 440s and the Hemi came standard with TorqueFlite automatic. Ordering the four-speed brought a pistol-grip Hurst shifter and a Dana 60 axle. Gear ratios climbed from 3.23:1 to 4.10:1, with limited-slip an extra-cost item. All R/Ts got a beefed suspension, and 440 and Hemi

cars got 15-inch 60-series tires, though such essentials as power steering and front disc brakes were optional.

The R/T's standard hood had two scoops that were open but didn't feed directly to the air cleaner. A $97 option was the shaker scoop, which mounted to the air cleaner and protruded through an opening in the hood. Full gauges, including a tach, were standard, and R/Ts could also be ordered in SE guise, which included leather seats and a vinyl roof with a smaller "formal" rear window.

Outward visibility was poor, and though everyday road manners were composed, the car felt bulky for its size. Hemis were quickest, but not by enough to justify their premium over the next-most-potent iteration, the 440 Six Pack. "With normal throttle it travels . . . with complete docility," *Road Test* said of its Six Pack Challenger. "The explosion comes when you stuff your foot down on the gas pedal, either on purpose or accidentally. The car squirts forward like an unleashed dragster . . . and suddenly you're way above the speed limit. . . . "

Specifications

1970 Dodge Challenger R/T 440 Six Pack

Wheelbase, in. 110.0

Weight, lbs. 3600

Production 1640

Price $5000

Engine ohv V-8

Displacement, cid 440

Fuel system 3 × 2bbl.

Compression ratio 10.5:1

Horsepower @ rpm 390 @ 4700

Torque @ rpm 490 @ 3200

Representative performance

0-60 mph, sec. 6.2

¼ mile, sec. @ mph 13.7 @ 105

Challenger shared a platform with the Plymouth Barracuda, but had a two-inch-longer wheelbase. R/Ts were the performance models. The optional 440 Six Pack used a trio of Holley two-barrels and open hood scoops. A tach was among the R/T's standard gauges, and the TorqueFlite was standard with the Hemi and 440 engines. Dodge sold 83,032 Challengers for '70. Of 19,938 R/Ts, 356 were Hemis, and 2035 were 440 Six Packs (including 99 ragtops and 296 SEs). This one is finished in Plum Crazy, one of Dodge's new extra-cost High Impact hues. Sub Lime, Go-Mango, and Top Banana were others.

1970 Dodge
Challenger T/A

W̲hen Dodge finally got a legitimate pony car to race in the Sports Car Club of America's Trans American Sedan Championship, it built a version for the street that went the competition car one wilder.

SCCA rules required Dodge to sell production editions of the track car, and Dodge responded with the Challenger T/A. The race cars ran a destroked 305-cid version of Mopar's fine 340-cid V-8. It had a four-barrel carb and some 440 bhp. Street T/As stayed with the 340, but upped the ante with a trio of two-barrel Holleys atop an Edelbrock aluminum intake manifold. Despite the "Six Pak" carburetion and a host of internal reinforcements, the T/A's mill carried the same 290 bhp rating as regular four-barrel 340s, though true output was near 350 bhp. Feeding it air was a suitcase-sized scoop molded into the pinned-down, lift-off matte-black fiberglass hood. Low-restriction dual exhausts ran to the stock muffler location under the trunk, then reversed direction to exit in chrome-tipped "megaphone" outlets in front of the rear wheels.

TorqueFlite automatic or Hurst-shifted four-speed, 3.55:1 or 3.90:1 gears, manual or power steering were available. Front discs were standard. The special Rallye suspension used heavy-duty everything and increased the camber of the rear springs. The T/A was among the first production cars with different sized tires front and rear: E60x15s up front, G60x15s in back. The modified camber elevated the tail enough to clear the rear rubber and the exhaust outlets, giving the T/A a real street-punk's stance. Thick side stripes, bold ID graphics, and a black ducktail spoiler joined the visual assault, though the cabin was standard Challenger R/T.

As it turned out, the T/A wasn't a consistent SCCA winner, and its street sibling didn't act much like a road racer, succumbing to debilitating understeer in fast corners. But the intensified 340 and meaty rear tires helped production versions claw through the quarter in the mid 14s, a showing that would do any small-block pony proud.

The T/A qualified racing Challengers for Trans Am competition, but unlike the 305-cid four-barrel track cars, it used a 340 with three two-barrel Holleys. Raked stance, wild graphics, and lift-off fiberglass hood with molded-in scoop were standard. The interior was stock Challenger. This T/A wears Panther Pink paint.

1970 Dodge
Charger R/T Hemi

Like a veteran heavyweight calling on all his tools to finish strong in the late rounds, the Charger R/T returned for the last year of its classic period with an unprecedented array of tricks.

A new chrome loop front bumper was echoed by a fresh full-width taillamp housing, and R/T versions gained a simulated reverse body-side scoop. The color palette took on a younger look, borrowing high-impact hues like Plum Crazy and Go-Mango from the new Challenger. New front seats were the car's first to qualify as true buckets, and a hip pistol-grip handle now topped the available four-speed's Hurst shifter. Carried over was the extra-cost SE (Special Edition) group with its leather upholstery. And for the first time, Charger could be optioned with an electric sliding sunroof.

Again standard on the R/T was the 375-bhp 440-cid four-barrel, but for those who didn't wish to shell out another $648 for the 425-bhp 426 Hemi, there was a new choice, the 390-bhp 440 with a trio of Holley two-barrels. Its cost and upkeep were friendlier than the Hemi's, torque was identical (at 800 less rpm), and in a street fight, few big cars were tougher than a 440 Six Pack. King Kong itself grew more accommodating with the addition of hydraulic lifters, which were better than solid tappets at maintaining the valve lash so essential for good Hemi performance. Still, being fast with a Hemi required keeping all four carburetor barrels from opening until the tires hooked up. Not every driver was so skillful. "If you were Hemi hunting in a lesser car, you wanted to catch him at a stop," explained Patrick Bedard in his 1990 *Car and Driver* "street warriors" retrospective. "If he fumbled and you were lucky enough to pull out a fender-length on him, you claimed victory early by backing off the power, thereby ending the run. If you were crazy enough to stay on it, the Hemi would take over in short order."

No Charger offered a broader array of thrills and frills than the '70. But rising insurance rates and tougher competition caused R/T sales to fall 50 percent, to 10,337, for the model year. With 116 orders, the new Six Pack outsold the Hemi by more than two to one.

This R/T displays a spectrum of Charger features for '70. It has the dual-quad 426 Hemi, the Special Edition package with leather upholstery, the new power sliding sunroof in a vinyl-covered top, and a pistol-grip handle for the Hurst-shifted four-speed. Front bumper, taillamps, and simulated side scoops were new this year.

Specifications

1970 Dodge Charger R/T SE Hemi

Wheelbase, in. 117.0

Weight, lbs. 4350

Production 42

Price $5600

Engine ohv V-8

Displacement, cid 426

Fuel system 2 × 4bbl.

Compression ratio 10.25:1

Horsepower @ rpm 425 @ 5000

Torque @ rpm 490 @ 4000

Representative performance

0-60 mph, sec. 5.5

¼ mile, sec. @ mph 13.9 @ 105

1970 Ford
Mustang Boss 302

*I*f Ford was embarrassed that its finest Mustangs were the handiwork of the same guys who developed the best Camaros, it certainly never said so. Revenge is sweet.

GM executive Semon "Bunkie" Knudsen, who used performance to revive Pontiac, defected to become president of Ford in early 1968. He brought along stylist Larry Shinoda, whose work included the Z28 that had unseated Mustang as '68 and '69 Trans Am champ. The Mach 1 was among their first efforts, but the most-special '69 and '70 Mustangs drew on Shinoda's nickname for Knudsen, "boss."

Like the Z28, the Boss 302 was built as a Trans Am road-racing qualifier. Its heart was Ford's 302-cid V-8 treated to the high-performance, big-port cylinder heads being readied for the famous Cleveland 351. The Boss's solid-lifter small-block used the biggest carb employed by Ford, a 780-cfm Holley four-barrel, and was underrated at the same 290 bhp as the Z28's 302. A Hurst-shifted four speed and 3.50:1 gears were stan-

dard; 3.91:1 and Detroit Locker 4.30:1 cogs were optional. Underneath were racing-inspired suspension modifications, Polyglas F60x15s, and power front discs.

Shinoda's expertise in aerodynamics influenced the Boss's exterior. Mustang's phony fender vents were enclosed and a front spoiler was fitted; a rear air foil and backlight blinds were optional. Blackout trim and stripes finished the look. Ford built 1628 Boss 302s for '69, then came back with 7013 for '70, when quad headlamps were traded for double units flanked by fake air intakes, a "shaker" hood scoop was made available, and the engine got smaller intake valves and a 6000-rpm rev limiter.

In Trans Am, racing Boss 302s retook the '70 crown from Chevy. Street versions weren't always as fast as a 302 Z28, but they had more cornering power and a less-peaky, more-flexible engine. "The Boss 302 is a hell of an enthusiasts's car," said *Car and Driver.* "It's what the Shelby GT 350s and 500s should have been but weren't."

Specifications
1970 Ford Mustang Boss 302

Wheelbase, in. 108.0

Weight, lbs. 3420

Production 7013

Price $4100

Engine ohv V-8

Displacement, cid 302

Fuel system 1 × 4bbl.

Compression ratio 10.5:1

Horsepower @ rpm 290 @ 5800

Torque @ rpm 290 @ 4300

Representative performance

0-60 mph, sec. 6.5

¼ mile, sec. @ mph 14.8 @ 96

Ford's answer to the Camaro Z28 was the Boss 302. Like the Chevy, it was built to qualify Trans Am racing versions and used a fortified 302-cid four-barrel V-8 rated at 290 bhp. The Boss 302 was launched for '69, and returned for '70 in greater numbers. All Boss 302s had stiffened underpinnings and did away with the regular Mustang fastback's fake bodyside scoops. Rear spoiler and flip-up rear-window slats were optional. A Hurst-shifted four-speed was mandatory. The '70 had single headlamps flanked by simulated vents and could be ordered with a functional shaker scoop that mounted to the air cleaner and quivered with the engine.

1970 Ford
Torino Cobra

*J*udging from their newfound plumpness, Detroit's 1970 crop of intermediates were not only midsized, but middle aged. Nowhere was that truer than at Ford, where the Torino gained an inch of wheelbase and five full inches of length, making it among the very largest cars in the segment. At least the reshaped sheetmetal looked aero-inspired, while a two-inch increase in tread width allowed Ford to squeeze in a new high-performance engine.

Replacing the willing but aged 428-cid V-8 was a new 429-cid mill. This was not the semi-hemi Boss 429 engine, but a fresh design with thin-wall construction and canted-valve heads. Ford retained a familiar moniker for the hottest versions, and built a new muscle car around them: the Torino Cobra. This was basically a SportsRoof Tornio GT in fighting trim, with exposed headlamps, blackout hood, and available muscle-car touches like rear-window slats and fat Polyglas F60x15s on seven-inch-wide Magnum 500 wheels. Standard equipment included a Hurst-shifted four-speed, competition suspension with staggered rear shocks, and Cobra insignia.

The standard engine was a 10.5:1-compression 360-bhp version of the 429. Things quickly got serious with the 370-bhp Cobra variant, which had an 11.3:1 squeeze, different heads, a high-lift cam, and a 700-cfm Holley four-barrel on a high-rise manifold. With the available shaker scoop, this engine was called the 429 Cobra Jet Ram-Air, but stayed at 370 bhp. Ordering the Drag Pack with the Cobra engine added Traction-Lok 3.91:1 or Detroit Locker 4.30:1 gears, a mechanical-lifter cam, oil cooler, forged aluminum pistons, four-bolt mains, and a 780-cfm four-barrel, for a 375-bhp rating. (Early '70 ads also listed the genuine Boss 429 as a Torino Cobra option, though few were installed.)

Tornio Cobras weren't as brutally overpowering as some rival big-blocks, but they were strong enough on the street. Part of the car's heft actually helped performance: With so much weight in the tail, dig off the line was excellent and its 0-60 mph sprints were extremely competitive. Handling was surprisingly composed, comfort was high, and Cobras—those without solid lifters—were quiet. Evidently, middle age has its good points.

Specifications

1970 Ford Torino Cobra

Wheelbase, in. 117.0

Weight, lbs. 4000

Production 7675

Price $4200

Engine ohv V-8

Displacement, cid 429

Fuel system 1 × 4bbl.

Compression ratio 11.3:1

Horsepower @ rpm 370 @ 5400

Torque @ rpm 450 @ 3400

Representative performance

0-60 mph, sec. 6.0

¼ mile, sec. @ mph 13.99 @ 101

Cobra still was a serious muscle car, but it now was confined to Torino SportsRoof styling in a larger, redesigned body. A 429-cid V-8 was standard, and the new 370-bhp Cobra version could get the optional shaker scoop. A T-handle Hurst-shifted four-speed was standard. Cobra's odd horizontal-readout tachometer was left of the steering wheel. Rear-window slats were a popular option.

1970 Mercury Cyclone Spoiler

Mercury marched lockstep with Ford through much of the muscle age. Sure, it got many of the company's hot engines, but its Cougar never really ran with the wild ponies, and its midsize models were little more than fancy Fairlanes. That changed with the 1970 intro of the marque's best-ever performance car, the Cyclone Spoiler.

Here, finally was a body unique from that of the fastback Fords, a Coke-bottle shape with an individualized flavor. The Spoiler was the pure-performance version of the Cyclone GT, and actually came better equipped for battle than its Ford Torino Cobra cousin. Standard in the Mercury was the 370-bhp ram-air 429-cid V-8, an extra-cost upgrade in the Cobra. A Hurst-stirred four-speed with 3.50:1 Traction-Lok gears completed the drivetrain, while a "competition" handling package and G70x14 tires laced it down. As in the Ford, a Select-Shift automatic was optional, and so was the Drag Pack, which emboldened the 429 with solid lifters, stronger internals, and 375 bhp. The Drag Pack included 3.91:1 or 4.30:1 axles, the latter a Detroit Locker. As with the Torino

Cobra, the Boss 429 engine was advertised as an early Cyclone Spoiler option, but few, if any, were installed.

Spoiler didn't use a shaker hood, going instead with an integrated functional scoop. A chin spoiler and rear air foil were standard, and while exterior adornment was left to simple tape stripes, six "Grabber" colors (blue, orange, yellow, green, coral, and platinum) were available. Mercury went Ford one better on the inside, providing Cyclones with a standard instrument cluster that included a proper round tachometer, and oil pressure, coolant temperate and amp gauges, all angled toward the driver. Torino made do with idiot lights and a weird horizontal-reading tachometer.

Befitting a Mercury, the Cyclone Spoiler was a *big* car. It shared Torino's wheelbase, but at a rangy 209.9 inches, its body was longer than the Ford's by 3.7 inches. And it weighed about 100 pounds more, similarly equipped. But finally, here was something more than a Fairlane facsimile, here was a real muscle Mercury.

Specifications

1970 Mercury Cyclone Spoiler

Wheelbase, in. 117.0

Weight, lbs. 4100

Production 1631

Price $4300

Engine ohv V-8

Displacement, cid 429

Fuel system 1 × 4bbl.

Compression ratio 11.3:1

Horsepower @ rpm 370 @ 5400

Torque @ rpm 450 @ 3400

Representative performance

0-60 mph, sec. 6.2

¼ mile, sec. @ mph 14.1 @ 100

Mercury pulled itself out from under Ford's muscle shadow with the '70 Cyclone Spoiler. It was the same in spirit as the Torino Cobra, but its styling was distinct and its standard engine was the 370-bhp Ram Air 429 that cost extra on the Ford. Front and rear spoilers were included, as was a functional hood scoop (the shaker wasn't offered). A rim-blow horn, Hurst-shifted four-speed, high-back bucket seats, and a proper round tachometer and ancillary gauges angled toward the driver were standard.

1970 Oldsmobile 4-4-2 W-30

*T*ruth be told, the 1968 and '69 4-4-2 400-cid V-8 was a troubled motor. Olds had revised its bore and stroke to meet emissions and cost requirements, resulting in a "high-performance" mill that wouldn't rev past 5700 rpm and had subpar durability.

W-30 versions, benefitting from better-breathing heads and what amounted to factory blueprinting, matched the performance of the short-stroke '66-67 4-4-2 V-8s. But it wasn't until '70 that Olds got it together with perhaps the best all-around 4-4-2 ever.

The major advance was the newly standard 455-cid V-8, an under-stressed, big-port engine with tug-boat torque. Yet, it also had an advanced design that kept its exterior dimensions compact and its weight below that of the '69 400-cid V-8. It made 365 bhp in base form and was underrated at 370 in W-30 guise. The W-30 package again included what Olds called "Select Fit" engine parts, plus a performance calibrated four-barrel, a hotter cam, and low-restriction exhausts. A Hurst-managed four speed with 3.42:1 gears or a performance-calibrated Turbo

Hydra-matic 400 with a Hurst Dual-Gate shifter and 3.23:1 cogs were drivetrain choices. The Anti-Spin axle was standard and dealer-installed ratios up to 5.00:1 were available. Front disc brakes (with no power assist on four-speed cars), sway bars fore and aft, and G70x14 white-letter tires were other W-30 components.

Drawing on experience with 455-cid V-8s in Hurst-doctored cars, Olds knew what it took to get the engine to perform in a 4-4-2. Weight reduction was essential, as illustrated in the W-30 package. The hood, with molded-in functional scoops, was made of fiberglass and was 18 pounds lighter than the steel version. The W-30's intake manifold was aluminum, its inner fender liners were plastic, and the cars had less sound deadener than other 4-4-2s. Aluminum was even used for the differential carrier and cover, shaving another 18 pounds.

Oldsmobile's 1970 W-30s blended a plush bucket-seat cabin with athletic road manners and vivid acceleration. It was the thinking-man's approach to muscle.

Specifications

1970 Oldsmobile 4-4-2 W-30

Wheelbase, in. 112.0

Weight, lbs. 4200

Production 2574

Price $4900

Engine ohv V-8

Displacement, cid 455

Fuel system 1 × 4bbl.

Compression ratio 10.5:1

Horsepower @ rpm 370 @ 5200

Torque @ rpm 500 @ 3600

Representative performance

0-60 mph, sec. 5.7

¼ mile, sec. @ mph 14.2 @ 100

Olds made its 455-cid V-8 standard in the '70 4-4-2, and the W-30 package returned as the hot setup. The $321 option included a factory-blueprinted 370-bhp mill and weight-cutting tricks that included a fiberglass hood, red plastic inner front-fender liners, and, as seen at top left, an aluminum differential carrier and cover. In '70, W-30s were ordered on 2574 of 14,709 4-4-2 hardtops built, 262 of 1688 pillared coupes, and 264 of 2933 convertibles.

1970 Plymouth
Hemi 'Cuda

While Dodge went with big-car styling cues for its new pony, Plymouth favored a certain economy of line. The Barracuda may have looked lean, but with the right engine, it could be very mean.

Sporting derivations again were 'Cudas and featured five hot V-8s, from the sharp 275-bhp 340 and flexible 335-bhp 383, to the imposing 375-bhp four-barrel 440 and the brutal 390-bhp 440+6. Atop the list: the merciless 425-bhp 426 Hemi.

Plymouth knew the big-blocks' mission, and gave the 440 and Hemi 'Cudas a suspension tailored to heavy-metal acceleration. They had no aft stabilizer bar, but their rear leaf springs numbered five on the right, six on the left, with thicknesses chosen to equalize tire loads in hole shots. Wheel hop was negligible, but careless starts would still send the skins (F70x14s on 440s, F60x15s on Hemis) up in smoke.

The Barracuda rode a two-inch shorter wheelbase than the Challenger, though its body dimensions were the same. The 'Cuda's standard hood had phony intakes, but the functional shaker scoop was included with the Hemi and was a $97 option on other 'Cudas. Mopar gave the Hemi hydraulic lifters for '70, so it was easier to maintain and, according to some testers, had improved low-rpm power. Some also were impressed with the Hemi car's handling, though others said it was hopelessly nose-heavy. All agreed that ordering the optional 11.3-inch front disc brakes was a smart move. But which 'Cuda was quickest?

Compared to the $871 Hemi, the 440+6 was a bargain at $250. Both came with a Hurst pistol-grip four-speed or Slap-Stik TorqueFlite and an extra-heavy duty Dana axle. Both had quirks that could make for an interesting drive to the supermarket: The six-barrel's vacuum-actuated front and rear carbs came on with little warning, while the Hemi's stiff throttle linkage sometimes snapped all eight barrels open at once.

The 440+6 was easier to tune than a Hemi, and could stay with one to 70 mph or so. That might be enough away from a stoplight. But not in really serious action, where the relentless race-bred 426 was in its element. Nobody handed this engine its reputation. It earned it.

Specifications

1970 Plymouth Hemi 'Cuda

Wheelbase, in. 108.0

Weight, lbs. 3900

Production 652

Price $5400

___

Engine ohv V-8

Displacement, cid 426

Fuel system 2 × 4bbl.

Compression ratio 10.25:1

Horsepower @ rpm 425 @ 5000

Torque @ rpm 490 @ 4000

Representative performance

___

0-60 mph, sec. 5.6

¼ mile, sec. @ mph 13.41 @ 104.6

The redesigned '70 Barracuda was one the prettiest pony cars—and 'Cuda versions were among the most-potent. Just 652 hardtops (of 17,242 built) and 14 convertibles (of 550) got the Hemi engine. Its standard shaker scoop mounted to the air cleaner and fed fresh air to big dual quads. The sporty interior included full gauges; four-speed models got Mopar's cool pistol-grip shifter.

1970 Plymouth AAR 'Cuda

Of course, the production AAR 'Cuda couldn't be mechanically identical to its Trans-Am racing namesake. But unlike the Mustang Boss 302 and Camaro Z28, which also were built to homologate track cars, it didn't even try to mimic the pavement-hugging posture of its competition cousin. What Plymouth built was a street rod.

The AAR 'Cuda took its title from Dan Gurney's All-American Racers, the team that campaigned Barracudas in the Sports Car Club of America's popular competition series. Like the similar racing Dodge Challenger T/As, track AARs ran full-race 440-bhp 305-cid four-barrel V-8s and were lowered and modified for all-out twisty-course combat. And like production Challenger T/As built to qualify the cars for racing, street AARs used a 290-bhp 340-cid with three two-barrel Holley carbs on an Edelbrock aluminum manifold. Buyers could choose a four-speed or TorqueFlite, with a Sure-Grip axle and standard 3.55:1 or optional 3.91:1 gears. The engine breathed through a functional hood scoop.

The AAR's interior was basic 'Cuda, but its exterior certainly was not. From a matte-black lift-off fiberglass hood, through body-side strobe stripes and tri-colored AAR shield, to the standard black ducktail spoiler, this was an exotic fish. Special shocks and recambered rear springs raised the tail 1¾ inches over regular 'Cuda specs, allowing clearance for exhausts pipes that exited in front of the rear wheelwell (after routing through the standard muffler beneath the trunk). It also permitted use of G60x15 tires in back and E60x15s in front.

With its raked stance, oversized rear rubber, side-exit exhausts, and loud graphics, an AAR was better suited to a Saturday night at Burger King than a Sunday afternoon at Lime Rock. With a 56-percent-front weight bias, handling was plagued by understeer, prompting *Car and Driver* to suggest "it might have been better to put the fat tires on the front wheels." But the AAR 'Cuda was strong in a straight line, and an eyeful anywhere. Just like a good street rod.

Cousin to Dodge's Challenger T/A was the AAR 'Cuda. Both were built for 1970 to qualify Trans Am racing versions. Side-exit exhaust tips, audacious graphics, bold fiberglass hood, and raked stance (with oversized rear tires) gave it a cocksure attitude, one reinforced by such High-Impact colors as Lemon Twist, In-Violet, and Tor-Red. The AAR handled nothing like its racing namesake, but its tri-carb 340-cid V-8 made it a straight-line achiever.

Specifications
1970 Plymouth AAR 'Cuda

Wheelbase, in. 108.0

Weight, lbs. 3600

Production 2724

Price $4340

Engine ohv V-8

Displacement, cid 340

Fuel system 3 × 2bbl.

Compression ratio 10.5:1

Horsepower @ rpm 290 @ 5000

Torque @ rpm 345 @ 3400

Representative performance

0-60 mph, sec. 5.8

¼ mile, sec. @ mph 14.4 @ 99.5

1970 Plymouth
Duster 340

Just as it had with the Road Runner in '68, Plymouth scored a budget-muscle bull's-eye in 1970 with the Duster 340. The formula was familiar. Take a cheap-to-produce platform, in this case a Valiant wearing a new fastback body, and treat it to a hot engine, here Mopar's respected 340-cid four-barrel V-8.

The determined little Duster was lighter, roomier, and faster than the 340 'Cuda. With a base price of just $2547, it was the lowest-priced car in Plymouth's Rapid Transit System. And it was the only one with front disc brakes standard.

The 340 V-8 had proven itself over preceding years, propelling a series of giant-killer Darts and earlier-generation Barracudas to mid-14-second ETs at near 100 mph. It used a Carter AVS four-barrel and camshaft timing only slightly less radical than that of the mighty 440 Six Pack. It was rated at 275 bhp, but practiced observers insisted it actually made closer to 325 bhp. In the Duster, the engine came with a heavy-duty three-speed manual or a choice of optional four-speed or

TorqueFlite. A 3.23:1 axle was standard; 3.55:1 and 3.91:1 gears, plus a Sure-Grip limited-slip diff, were available at extra cost.

Since it was a member of the Rapid Transit System, the Duster 340 was treated to an array of performance enhancers, including heavy-duty underpinnings, front stabilizer bar, and six-leaf rear springs. Standard tires were E70x14s on 5.5-inch rally wheels. It borrowed the instrument panel from the earlier-series Barracuda, and bucket seats and a center console with floor shift could be ordered in place of the front bench. A pistol-grip for the four-speed, an 8000-rpm tach, and power steering were attractive extra-cost items. No scoops were offered, and the only hot-car cues were dual exhausts and modest decals.

The stiff, slightly lowered suspension made for a punishing ride and didn't prevent the car's nose from plowing through fast corners. And with the cut-rate price came some obviously low-budget trim. But the Duster 340 was reasonably fast, it was utilitarian, it was a bit of a sleeper, and it had character. Bull's-eye!

Based on the new Valiant-based fastback, Plymouth's Duster 340 was a sort of pocket Road Runner. It had the scrappy 340-cid V-8, a beefed drivetrain, and a heavy-duty suspension, but no boy-racer scoops or spoilers. Options such as bucket seats, console, and TorqueFlite shown here dress up what was otherwise a decidedly low-budget cabin. This car's extra-cost High Impact color was called Panther Pink by Dodge, Moulin Rouge by Plymouth.

1970 Plymouth
Road Runner Hemi

*O*ne of the treats of the muscle age was muscle marketing. Never had Detroit so brazenly broken from conservative advertising themes to embrace the spirit of the moment.

Some of the ads were full of bravado. "We'll take on any other two cars in the magazine," said one Chevy tag line under the photo of a Camaro SS and a Corvette. Others aimed at cleverness, such as one picturing a striped tail caught under the closed hood of a Ford Fairlane GT and the come-on "How to cook a tiger."

But the most entertaining were those from Dodge and Plymouth. Rife with op-art graphics, flower-power imagery, and brilliant colors, they were an unabashed reflection of the times. The '70 Road Runner, for example, was introduced with a photo showing a giant, three-dimensional sculpture of its goofy cartoon namesake emerging from a trap door on the hood.

The tag line, "The loved bird," was both a wry play on words and an accurate reflection of the car's popularity. Sales for '69 had doubled those of '68, sparking a legion of imitators. The photo, besides being funny, also illustrated a functional new feature, the Air Grabber hood.

This was the year Plymouth grouped its meanest cars under the "Rapid Transit System" banner. The redesigned 'Cuda and the new Duster 340 were charter members, while the Road Runner and GTX celebrated with freshened styling, including handsome loop-motif front and rear ends and dummy rear-fender scoops. Powertrains were basically unchanged, though the 426 Hemi engine went from solid to hydraulic lifters in the interest of greater durability and cleaner emissions, and the Road Runner's standard four-speed manual moved to the options list, replaced by a heavy-duty three-speed.

That Air Grabber hood was standard with the Hemi and available with either 440. The driver would trip an underdash switch, causing the power-operated trap door to rise slowly, revealing a planed-off scoop with a snarling shark cartoon painted on its side. Just the thing for psyching out the opposition at stoplights.

Plymouth's intermediates finished their 1968-70 styling cycle with freshened sheetmetal and a revised dashboard. Road Runner sales slipped to about 39,600 for '70, of which 75 hardtops, 74 pillared coupes, and three convertibles got the optional 426 Hemi engine. The Air Grabber hood with its power-operated trap door and snarling-shark graphics was new. The source of the car's whimsical "beep-beep" horn sound was a purple underhood module.

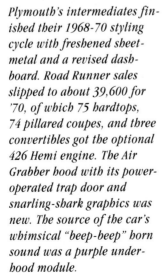

1970 Pontiac
Firebird Trans Am

*F*irebird and Camaro grew more European in nature with their second-generation redesign, but the scooped and spoilered Trans Am was pure American muscle, and more immodest than ever.

Its standard V-8, the 345-bhp Ram Air 400-cid, furnished low-14-second ETs. That apparently satisfied most buyers, because just 88 of 3196 Trans Ams built for '70 got the optional Ram Air IV. That one added bigger ports, better heads, swirl-polished valves, and an aluminum intake manifold, for 370 bhp, 25 more than in '69. Rarer still was the Ram Air V, an over-the-counter, special-order piece that counted among its tricks solid lifters and tunnel-port heads for as much as 500 bhp. All these engines breathed through a new rear-facing shaker scoop designed to capture cool ambient air flowing over the hood. A four-speed with Hurst shifter was standard, Turbo Hydra-matic was optional. Both came with 3.55:1 gears, and a 3.73:1 was available with the four-speed.

Road manners received much attention. The padded Formula steering wheel directed quick 12.1:1 variable-ratio power steering. Stiffer springs and heavy-duty front and rear sway bars teamed with Polyglas F60x15 tires on Kelsey Hayes Rally II wheels. Standard 10.9-inch power front disc brakes and 9.5-inch rear drums did the stopping.

Trans Am wore the same impact-absorbing snout as other Firebirds, but Pontiac said its unique front air dam and fender air extractors created 50 pounds of downforce on the nose at expressway speeds. It claimed equal downforce to the tail from a big decklid lip and small spoilers in front of the rear wheels. Inside, complete instrumentation was standard and included a tachometer turned on its side to redline at 12 o'clock, just like in a real race car.

Critics were impressed. Even with 57 percent of the weight on the front wheels, *Sport Car Graphic* said, "Overall handling feel—for a production car—was as near to a front engine race car as we have ever driven." And *Car and Driver* called the '70 Trans Am "a hard muscled, lightning-flexed commando of a car, the likes of which doesn't exist anywhere in the world, even for twice the price."

Specifications

1970 Pontiac Trans Am Ram Air IV

Wheelbase, in. 108.0

Weight, lbs. 3900

Production 88

Price $4600

Engine ohv V-8

Displacement, cid 400

Fuel system 1 × 4bbl.

Compression ratio 10.5:1

Horsepower @ rpm 370 @ 5500

Torque @ rpm 445 @ 3900

Representative performance

0-60 mph, sec. 5.6

¼ mile, sec. @ mph 13.9 @ 102

With introduction of the second-generation Firebird, Pontiac's Trans Am came into its own as a bare-knuckles brawler. Functional spoilers and vents abounded, while super-tough underpinnings and quickened steering gave it corner-hungry handling. Only the strongest 400-cid V-8s were offered. This is the 370-bhp Ram Air IV; its rear-facing fresh-air scoop worked. The standard thick-rimmed Formula steering wheel, bucket seats, engine-turned instrument surround, and full gauges made for a purposeful cabin.

1970 Pontiac GTO Judge

*P*ontiac altered the GTO's styling for 1970, giving it a new Endura nose with exposed headlamps, bodyside creases, and a revised rump. Underhood, a newly optional 360-bhp 455-cid V-8 provided 500 lb-ft of torque at just 3100 rpm, perfect for the option-laden, luxury tourers many Goats had become.

Pontiac kept the Judge focused on performance. The 455 was off its docket until the last quarter of the model year, when it became available via special order. Most got the 366-bhp 400-cid Ram Air III mill. The extra-cost 370-bhp Ram Air IV was installed in a relative handful.

Few cars made a bolder visual statement. "The Judge" decals returned, multi-hued stripes appeared over the bodyside creases, and the 60-inch rear wing now stood high and proud on the tail. Some Judges also got a matte-black fiberglass chin spoiler. Orbit-Orange remained an exclusive Judge color, and was teamed with combination blue/orange/pink stripes. "The Judge," observed *Road Test* magazine, "is not for people who are shy about being looked at."

But there was no shortage of substance here. Both 400-cid V-8s came with functional hood scoops (an underdash knob controlled air flow). Pontiac finally made a rear sway bar standard, and sharpened handling further with a beefier front bar, softer springs, and revised shock valving. The introduction of variable-ratio power steering also improved response.

Transmission choices mirrored those of regular Goats: three-speed manual standard, four-speed and automatic optional, with four-speed Judges getting a Hurst T-handle shifter. Interiors also were standard GTO, except for Judge insignia.

Sales of the '70 Judge declined with those of the GTO, and by mid '71, skidding demand caused Pontiac to retire the special edition after selling just 357 hardtops and 17 ragtops. By then, the top GTO engine was a 335-bhp 455 with 8.4:1 compression. For '72, the proud Goat was once again a LeMans option. It would die ignominiously as a '74 Ventura trim package. The GTO was the original muscle car, and the Judge was the GTO at its most extroverted.

Specifications

1970 Pontiac GTO Judge

Wheelbase, in. 112.0

Weight, lbs. 4000

Production 168

Price $4800

Engine ohv V-8

Displacement, cid 400

Fuel system 1 × 4bbl.

Compression ratio 10.5:1

Horsepower @ rpm 366 @ 5100

Torque @ rpm 445 @ 3600

Representative performance

0-60 mph, sec. 6.0

¼ mile, sec. @ mph 14.7 @ 98

As the GTO evolved into a luxury-muscle intermediate, the Judge clung to its adolescent roots. Graphics and wings were wilder for '70, and the 455 V-8 was delayed in favor of Ram Air 400s; their foam gasket sealed to the hood scoops. This Ram Air III car has the optional Formula steering wheel and four-speed with Hurst T-handle shifter. The Judge was a $337 option for '70, and of 3797 built, just 168 were ragtops.

1971 AMC
Hornet SC/360

*E*ven in 1970, muscle's pinnacle year, the signs were there for those who chose to look. Federal safety watchdogs, state and national emissions regulators, insurance companies—even a changing social climate—all took aim at the high-performance car. For '71, the shots began to hit the target. Compression ratios retreated to accommodate regular-grade fuel, gross horsepower ratings began to fall to tamer-sounding net figures, and public relations-conscious automakers backpedaled.

Into this upheaval stepped AMC with a car that didn't deny the new reality. "Introducing a sensible alternative to the money-squeezing, insurance-strangling muscle cars of America," said its advertisement. "The Hornet SC/360." Hornet was the company's newest compact and the two-door sedan was a reasonable basis for a low-profile muscle car. Original plans called for both an SC/360 and an SC/401, but when AMC discovered that a 401-cid Hornet probably wouldn't provide much of

an insurance edge, the 360-cid V-8 alone was borrowed from the Javelin AMX. In standard form, it had a two-barrel carb and a modest 245 bhp. The $199 "Go" package included a four-barrel and a ram air setup for a more satisfying 285 bhp. These were gross ratings. Optional in place of the standard three-speed was a Hurst-shifted four-speed or an automatic. Polyglas D70x14s were standard, with upgrades running to the handling package and the Twin-Grip diff with 3.54:1 or 3.90:1 gears.

An SC/360 couldn't stay with the big-cube holdovers, but it did combine respectable quickness with a taut suspension, big tires, and modest size for a package praised by *Motor Trend* as "just a plain gas to drive . . . it handles like a dream."

The SC/360 turned out to be a sleeper in more ways than one. Even with a base price of just $2663 (about $40 below the '71 Duster 340), it made up only a fraction of the 75,000 Hornets built for '71. The SC/360 died after just one year as one of the muscle-era's better-kept secrets.

Specifications

1971 AMC SC/360

Wheelbase, in. 108.0

Weight, lbs. 3200

Production 784

Price $3000

Engine ohv V-8

Displacement, cid 360

Fuel system 1 × 4bbl.

Compression ratio 8.5:1

Horsepower @ rpm 285 @ 4800

Torque @ rpm 390 @ 3200

Representative performance

0-60 mph, sec. 6.7

¼ mile, sec. @ mph 14.9 @ 95

As the sun set on big-block intermediates, automakers turned to junior muscle cars. One of the quickest—and rarest—was AMC's SC/360. Based on the compact Hornet, it offered a 360-cid V-8 in 245-bhp two-barrel form or, as here, a 285-bhp ram-air four-barrel. With the optional Hurst-shifted four-speed, an SC/360 like this could turn high 14s. A sport suspension and efficient dimensions made it a pleasing handler.

1971 Buick GS 455

*T*he names hadn't changed, but the personalities had. There was still a GS 455, but instead of high-lift cams and tall numeric axles, there were low-compression engines and low-octane appetites. It wasn't alone.

GM said all its 1971 models must run on low-lead, regular-grade fuel (91 octane), and meet stricter exhaust-emission standards. The edict reduced the compression ratio of the GS 455's V-8 to 8.5:1, from 1970's 10.0:1. Horsepower tumbled along with it, to 315, from 350. The extra-cost Stage 1 package dropped two full points of compression and suffered a decline to 345 bhp from 360.

These were gross horsepower ratings. For '72, all the automakers would begin publishing net ratings that reflected engine output with all accessories in place. Though a given engine's actual output didn't change from '71 to '72, net figures made for some startling numbers. The '72 GS 455, for example, had a 250-bhp rating, the Stage 1, a 270.

While muscle's light was dimmed, all was not darkness. The '71 GS 455 still came with a four-barrel carb, dual exhausts, and functional hood scoops that fed the standard ram-air induction system. Heavy duty springs and shocks, wide-oval tires, and a front stabilizer bar were included in the base price, which rose nominally, to $3285 for the Sport Coupe and $3476 for the convertible. Styling was as aggressive as ever, and even the GSX returned, if only as an appearance option.

Three- and four-speed manuals and the automatic were back, though the 3.61:1 axle ratio was dropped and the 3.42:1 took over as the top factory gear. Any 455 still had enough torque for an impressive seat-of-the-pants feel under hard acceleration, but ETs don't lie, and the '71s were a second or more slower in the quarter than the '70s. GS sales plunged more than 50 percent for the year. The Gran Sport 455 would remain on the roster through 1974, then fade out as a grand remnant of Buick's big-block glory days.

Specifications

1971 Buick GS 455

Wheelbase, in. 112.0

Weight, lbs. 4150

Production 902

Price $3700

Engine ohv V-8

Displacement, cid 455

Fuel system 1 × 4bbl.

Compression ratio 8.5:1

Horsepower @ rpm 315 @ 4400

Torque @ rpm 450 @ 2800

Representative performance

0-60 mph, sec. 6.9

¼ mile, sec. @ mph 15.3 @ 96

To meet tougher exhaust-emissions standards and GM's new rule that all engines run on low-octane gas, Buick and its sister divisions lowered compression ratios of their performance mills to around 8.5:1. Power fell with it: The base GS 455 dropped to 315 bhp from 350, the Stage 1 to 345 from 360. Torque was still healthy, while ram air and a stout suspension kept the sporty feel intact. Still, GS 455 production dropped to 9170. This Bittersweet Mist ragtop is one of 902 GS 455 convertibles built for '71.

1971 Chevrolet
Chevelle SS 454

Quarter-mile times in the low-14s required no apology, but they weren't too impressive coming off a year in which the best Chevelles dipped into the low 13s. Chevrolet, like all of Detroit, was struggling to cope with a world that had changed overnight.

Emissions standards had forced a switch to low-lead fuel, which in turn cut compression ratios, while insurance surcharges on supercars prompted tamer power-to-weight ratios. The impact was obvious in the 1971 Chevelle SS line, where small-blocks re-emerged in the form of two 350-cid V-8s, a 245-bhp two-barrel and a 270-bhp four-barrel.

But big-block power still was available. The 402-cid four-barrel cost $173 and had 300 bhp, 50 bhp below the previous year's base SS engine. To retain the hallowed SS 396 badging, Chevy had called the 1970 402 a "396." For '71, it was renamed the "Turbo Jet 400."

Chevy had taunted enthusiasts with word that the majestic 454-cid LS6 would be back for '71. Compression would be a modest 9.0:1, but output a still-formidable 425 bhp. It was never released for public sale, however. Instead, the hydraulic-lifter LS5 returned as a $279 option on top of the basic SS package. Compression fell to 8.5:1, from 10.25:1, but bhp actually increased by five, to 365, though it peaked 600 rpm lower than in '70. Torque was down by 35 lb-ft. The LS5 was teamed with the Turbo Hydra-matic 400 or the M22 Rock Crusher four speed; 3.31:1 gears were standard, with a 4.10:1 Posi optional.

The basic SS package included a lot for its $357 price: the F41 suspension with front and rear stabilizer bars, power front discs, wider F60 tires on larger 15-inch five-spoke wheels, and blackout grille. All Chevelles got single headlamps borrowed from the Monte Carlo, and the SS could be spiffed with optional racing stripes and the extra-cost Cowl Induction hood. Interestingly, only LS5 cars carried external engine ID; their badges said "SS 454." All others wore simple "SS" insignia. That was a pretty revealing sign of the times.

Specifications

1971 Chevrolet Chevelle SS 454

Wheelbase, in. 112.0

Weight, lbs. 4000

Production 9502

Price $4700

Engine ohv V-8

Displacement, cid 454

Fuel system 1 × 4bbl.

Compression ratio 8.5:1

Horsepower @ rpm 365 @ 4800

Torque @ rpm 465 @ 3200

Representative performance

0-60 mph, sec. 6.0

¼ mile, sec. @ mph 14.35 @ 97

Buyers could get a 245-bhp 350 two-barrel (with single exhaust!) in a '71 Chevelle Super Sport, but the 454 returned for those who wouldn't knuckle under. The only version available was this 365-bhp LS5. Changed styling included single headlamps and new round taillamps, but only 454s displayed engine size along with their SS badges. Vinyl roof, styled steel wheels, and the $100 gauge group with sport steering wheel are among this hardtop's options. For '71, Chevy built 19,293 Chevelle SSs (including El Caminos); 9502 had the 454 V-8.

1971 Dodge
Charger R/T Hemi

With muscle in retreat, the last thing anyone would have expected to see on the order sheet was the 426 Hemi, but there it was. Granted, not many were delivered for '71, but that didn't mean the Hemi didn't still deliver.

Mopar was holding out better than most against the anti-performance onslaught. Compression ratios were down only fractionally, and horsepower cuts were not severe. The Hemi continued with a 10.25:1 squeeze and retained 425 bhp and 490 lb-ft of torque. Chrysler installed just 356 of the mills for '71, 186 of them in Dodge Challengers and Plymouth 'Cudas.

The balance was spread among the redesigned Plymouth Road Runner and GTX, and the new Dodge Charger and its close cousin, the Charger Super Bee. The '71 Charger was a radical departure from its predecessor, losing two inches of wheelbase and gaining swoopy Coke-bottle contours. It now shared its body with the Super Bee, and though its performance leader retained the R/T designation, the only '71

Charger to come standard with the car's trademark hidden headlamps was the luxury SE version; they were otherwise optional.

But the R/T stayed true to its roots with a daunting underhood lineup. The 370-bhp 440-cid four-barrel Magnum V-8 was standard, with the 385-bhp 440 Six Pack available at extra cost. Topping the roster was the Hemi, which cost $884, not including required extras such as the Sure-Grip diff. A four-speed was standard, TorqueFlite was optional, and Hemi Chargers fed their dual quads with an Air Grabber-type hood scoop activated by a dashboard switch.

A standard blackout hood, simulated bodyside air extractors, Rallye wheels, tape stripes, and optional front and rear spoilers made this the most garish Charger ever, particularly when swathed in extra-cost colors like "Green Go" and "Citron Yella." Charger retained this body style through 1974, but would never again have a Hemi. Chrysler dropped the historic engine from the regular-production roster after this year, making 1971 the requiem for this heavyweight.

Specifications

1971 Dodge Charger R/T Hemi

Wheelbase, in. 115.0

Weight, lbs. 4000

Production 63

Price $5800

Engine ohv V-8

Displacement, cid 426

Fuel system 2 × 4bbl.

Compression ratio 10.25:1

Horsepower @ rpm 425 @ 5000

Torque @ rpm 490 @ 4000

Representative performance

0-60 mph, sec. 5.8

¼ mile, sec. @ mph 13.7 @ 104

Charger lost an inch of its wheelbase, three inches of overall length, and its handsome styling for '71. Instrumentation and ergonomics improved, but hidden headlamps were now optional on all but the luxury SE version. The R/T returned, and 63 of the 3118 built were ordered with the 426 Hemi, which included a flip-up hood scoop. Of 5054 Charger Super Bees, 22 were Hemis. The legendary engine was dropped after this year.

1971 Ford
Mustang Boss 351

*F*ord's decade of "Total Performance" was rapidly drawing to a close, but something was still kicking in the stall: the Boss 351.

Based on the redesigned Mustang SportsRoof, the new Boss was built to qualify a Trans-Am counterpart, a purpose rendered moot by Ford's late-1970 retirement from most forms of organized racing. The upside was that the Boss 351 was probably the only 1971 performance car with a genuine competition-grade engine.

Unfortunately, it had to saddle up the biggest Mustang ever. Wheelbase was up one inch, and the car gained 2.1 inches in overall length, 2.8 inches in width, and put on about 100 pounds. Its styling was influenced by the last of the Shelby models, which didn't survive into '71. That left the Mach 1 and Boss 351 as Mustang's similarly styled performance flag bearers.

Mach 1's top engine was the 429-cid Super Cobra Jet Ram Air. Its credentials were strong—11.3:1 compression, 375 bhp, 450 lb-ft of torque—but its low-14-second ETs were slower than those of the Boss

351. The Boss had on its side less weight and exclusive use of a thoroughbred 351-cid V-8 that *Car and Driver* said made the "Z/28 look like a gas mileage motor." Its rods were shotpeened and Magnafluxed and its heads, drawn from the Boss 302, had staggered valves and huge ports. It had a radical, solid-lifter cam, 11.0:1 compression, a 750-cfm four-barrel, and an honest 330 bhp. Ram-air induction, a Hurst-shifted four-speed, and a 3.91:1 Traction-Lok diff were standard.

The engine, remarkably tame on the street and a dervish on the track, teamed with a "competition" suspension that used F60x15 tires. Ultimate cornering power was high, but the car was ponderous and nowhere near as balanced as a Firebird Trans Am. Moreover, the cave-like cabin was frustratingly difficult to see out of, the ride was harsh, and the gauges and controls were poorly designed.

Mustang had gone from quarter horse to Clydesdale and its best version, Boss 351, lasted just one season. It was a fitting finish to Total Performance.

Specifications

1971 Ford Mustang Boss 351

Wheelbase, in. 109.0

Weight, lbs. 3600

Production 1806

Price $4900

Engine ohv V-8

Displacement, cid 351

Fuel system 1 × 4bbl.

Compression ratio 11.0:1

Horsepower @ rpm 330 @ 5400

Torque @ rpm 370 @ 4000

Representative performance

0-60 mph, sec. 5.8

¼ mile, sec. @ mph 13.9 @ 102

The last Boss was a restyled and enlarged SportsRoof Mustang. Its 330-bhp solid-lifter 351 with standard ram air and Hurst-stirred four-speed was one of Ford's best-ever performers, and the car was quicker and more tractable than the earlier Boss 302. But it had less character. With its low seating, unfriendly ergonomics, and vision-impeding sheetmetal, the new Boss felt ponderous.

1971 Oldsmobile 4-4-2 W-30

*T*he bloom was off the performance rose, especially at General Motors, and it took a determined assault on the order sheet to come up with a muscle car worthy of the name. Luckily, Olds still identified its strongest 4-4-2 by a single option code, W-30.

Except for new grille and taillamp inserts, the 4-4-2 was essentially unaltered from 1970, though the pillared coupe body was dropped. Bigger changes were underhood, where GM's ruling that all its cars reduce emissions and run on regular-grade fuel caused a compression-ratio cut in the 4-4-2's 455-cid V-8. What was 10.5:1 became 8.5:1, a drop *Motor Trend* said "was rather like hitting Dr. Oldsmobile with a malpractice suit. But there's still some soul left in Lansing, and despite all the furor, a 4-4-2 will still churn up all the smoke and fury the average muscle car driver could need and probably handle."

That certainly was true of a W-30. Regular 4-4-2 mills lost not only compression, but got a milder camshaft and some other detuning that dropped them to 340 bhp, from 365 (both gross ratings). W-30s again were factory blueprinted and those used with manual transmission re-

tained the hotter 1970 cam. Aluminum intake manifold, low restriction air cleaner and exhaust system, and air-induction hood continued as components of the $369 W-30 option. Gross output fell slightly less than on the base engine, to 350 bhp from 370.

Olds also began listing net output with all accessories in place. The regular 4-4-2 came in at 270 bhp, the W-30 at 300. That seemed tame compared to the giddy figures of just a year earlier, but in reality, net ratings more accurately reflected power available at the driving wheels. It also was true that torque, the most vital factor in acceleration, remained abundant.

But the decline in performance was unstoppable. The W-30 setup associated with blueprinted engines and banzai hole shots would last only through '72, though the name appeared on enthusiast-oriented Oldsmobiles for years to come. The 4-4-2 itself reverted to a Cutlass option after '71. "There's always been something special about 4-4-2s," *Motor Trend* said as the car was fading. "They seemed to be the subtle man's GTO...."

Specifications

1971 Oldsmobile 4-4-2 W-30

Wheelbase, in. 112.0

Weight, lbs. 4200

Production 110

Price $5100

Engine ohv V-8

Displacement, cid 455

Fuel system 1 × 4bbl.

Compression ratio 8.5:1

Horsepower @ rpm 350 @ 4700

Torque @ rpm 460 @ 3200

Representative performance

0-60 mph, sec. 6.5

¼ mile, sec. @ mph 14.8 @ 98

Olds warmed the chilly performance climate with the W-30 option, which included a fiberglass hood, functional scoops, and the factory-blueprinted 455-cid four-barrel rated at 350 bhp. For '71, Olds built 6285 4-4-2 hardtops, 810 with the W-30 package, and 1304 ragtops, 110 with the W-30. Strato bucket seats were 4-4-2 standards; among this car's options are automatic transmission with Hurst Dual-Gate shifter, power front discs, four-spoke steering wheel, and underdash eight-track tape player.

1971 Plymouth
GTX 440+6

*T*he GTX was among the precious few 1971 muscle cars that needed no excuses. It was bold, it was bad. Some said it was beautiful.

Once again, the GTX played upscale companion to the budget-muscle Road Runner. Both were part of Chrysler's revamped midsize line (which also included the Dodge Charger), and both got curvaceous new "fuselage" styling on a wheelbase one-inch shorter than before. With the new body came a three-inch increase in rear track, which benefited handling, plus a reconfigured interior with a more-comfortable driving position and superior ergonomics.

Although Mopar was the slowest of Detroit's Big Three to scale back, not all its V-8s escaped detuning. Road Runner's standard 383-cid four-barrel, for instance, lost 35 bhp. GTX engines, however, held out relatively unscathed. Compression ratios were shaved slightly, but the standard 440 four-barrel and the optional triple-two-barrel 440+6 lost only five bhp, to 370 and 385, respectively. The extra-cost and seldom-ordered 426 Hemi held fast at 425 bhp. Four-speeds and TorqueFlites, with axle ratios up to 4.10:1, were still available, as was the Air Grabber hood.

Weight was up by about 170 pounds, however, and quarter-mile times crept higher, by nearly a full second in some tests. The '71 GTX also had the stiffest suspension rates of any Mopar intermediate, and while handling was adequate, most testers concluded that it wasn't good enough to justify the rock-hard ride. But clearly, there was sinew beneath that new skin, and the car could still scale muscle's twin peaks: under 14 seconds and over 100 mph in the quarter-mile.

"All in all," said *Car and Driver*, "we would have to say that the Plymouth GTX is a step forward on a front where all others are retreating. In certain areas, styling and driver comfort, for example, it is vastly improved over the previous model and only in performance, primarily because of increased weight, has it lost ground."

As it turned out, the GTX succumbed sooner rather than later to the forces killing hot machinery; 1971 was its last year. The more-popular Road Runner name lived on until the 1975 model year, but mostly as a muscle car in memory only. The GTX, at least, died with its big-cube boots on.

Specifications
1971 Plymouth GTX 440+6

Wheelbase, in. 115.0

Weight, lbs. 4000

Production 135

Price $3800

Engine ohv V-8

Displacement, cid 440

Fuel system 3 × 2bbl.

Compression ratio 10.3:1

Horsepower @ rpm 385 @ 4700

Torque @ rpm 490 @ 3200

Representative performance

0-60 mph, sec. 5.7

¼ mile, sec. @ mph 13.7 @ 102

Chrysler was slow to defuse its muscle cars, as evidenced by the still-formidable tri-carb 440. It was available in re-designed Dodge and Plymouth intermediates, and put teeth into that pop-up hood scoop. Cabins of the '71s were sporty and functional, while a wider rear track improved handling. GTX production was just 2626, of which 135 got the 440+6 and 30 got the Hemi. Production of the similar Road Runner totalled 13,046, and 246 had the 440+6, 55 had the Hemi. Both the GTX and the Hemi were shelved after this year.

1971 Pontiac
Firebird Trans Am

*T*he 1971 Trans Am eclipsed the GTO as Pontiac's premier performance offering, and sent the rest of the pony field scurrying. Its weapon was the biggest V-8 ever offered in the class.

With just half-a-year production under its belt, Pontiac decided not to tamper with the appearance of the '71 Firebird, so Trans Am was visually unaltered, though new honeycomb wheels joined the options list. Still offered in just blue or white with contrasting stripes, the car kept its functional rear-facing shaker scoop. Like its sister divisions, Pontiac satisfied GM's new emissions policies by reducing compression ratios of existing engines. But instead of standing pat with a defused 400-cid V-8 for its new performance leader, the excitement division compensated for the cutbacks with a larger engine, the 455-cid V-8.

A 325-bhp version of the 455 was optional in the '71 Firebird Formula, but the 335-bhp 455 High Output was the only engine in the '71 Trans Am. To create the 455 HO, Pontiac borrowed the cylinder heads and camshaft from the previous year's 345-bhp Ram Air 400, and added the aluminum intake manifold from the rowdy 370-bhp 400 Ram Air IV. The 455 had less advertised power than the '70 T/A mills, and it couldn't wind as high. But at 8.4:1 compression (compared to 10.5:1 for the retired Ram Air 400s), it could run happily on a wider range of fuels, was less-temperamental than the Ram Air IV, and with 480 lb-ft of torque at a usable 3600 rpm, it packed a real wallop around town. Plus, it had four-bolt mains for strength.

A three-speed replaced the four-speed as the standard gear box; the four-speed (now with a larger clutch) and automatic cost extra. Factory axle ratios were a touch tamer, but a 3.73:1 was still available on cars without air conditioning. It all made for a Trans Am that was as quick as the best '70 models. Demand for such performance was about to bottom out. But among cars born of the muscle age, only Trans Am would continue in uninterrupted production. Pontiac always found a way.

With compression and horsepower falling all around it, Pontiac fought back, replacing Trans Am's peaky 400-cid stormers with a strong new 455-cid HO. It ran on low-octane gas, but had enough torque to furnish 1970-style acceleration. Trans Am retained its styling, its blue-and-white paint schemes, the ram air shaker scoop, and a state-of-the-art cabin, though honeycomb wheels were new. Sales fell to just 2116 units for '71. All had the 455 HO; this is one of 1231 ordered with automatic transmission.

Specifications

1971 Pontiac Firebird Trans Am

Wheelbase, in. 108.0

Weight, lbs. 3980

Production 2116

Price $4850

Engine ohv V-8

Displacement, cid 455

Fuel system 1 × 4bbl.

Compression ratio 8.4:1

Horsepower @ rpm 335 @ 4800

Torque @ rpm 480 @ 3600

Representative performance

0-60 mph, sec. 5.9

¼ mile, sec. @ mph 13.9 @ 103

Index